T0063030

The thought-provoking and tenacious

"So"

First of many links in the chain of
the "So, What"… series

Susan Chuey Williams Farah

A BOOK ABOUT

Discovery
Transformation
and Inspiration

BALBOA.
PRESS
A DIVISION OF HAY HOUSE

Copyright © 2014 Susan Chuey Williams Farah.

All rights reserved. No part of this book may be used or reproduced by any means, graphic, electronic, or mechanical, including photocopying, recording, taping or by any information storage retrieval system without the written permission of the publisher except in the case of brief quotations embodied in critical articles and reviews.

Balboa Press books may be ordered through booksellers or by contacting:

Balboa Press
A Division of Hay House
1663 Liberty Drive
Bloomington, IN 47403
www.balboapress.com
1 (877) 407-4847

Because of the dynamic nature of the Internet, any web addresses or links contained in this book may have changed since publication and may no longer be valid. The views expressed in this work are solely those of the author and do not necessarily reflect the views of the publisher, and the publisher hereby disclaims any responsibility for them.

The author of this book does not dispense medical advice or prescribe the use of any technique as a form of treatment for physical, emotional, or medical problems without the advice of a physician, either directly or indirectly. The intent of the author is only to offer information of a general nature to help you in your quest for emotional and spiritual well-being. In the event you use any of the information in this book for yourself, which is your constitutional right, the author and the publisher assume no responsibility for your actions.

Any people depicted in stock imagery provided by Thinkstock are models, and such images are being used for illustrative purposes only. Certain stock imagery © Thinkstock.

Printed in the United States of America.

ISBN: 978-1-4525-9584-9 (sc)
ISBN: 978-1-4525-9585-6 (e)

Library of Congress Control Number: 2014906535

Balboa Press rev. date: 06/18/2014

This Book is dedicated to:

Dottie and Johnnie who allowed me to be a kid long enough **so** I could learn to be a grown-up.

My sincere thanks to Claire, whose friendship and guidance made it possible for me to believe miracles could still happen.

To the angels-in-waiting who have crossed my path and helped steer me back.

Contents

Prologue

It's funny how life works.

You muddle through and it's only after you have lived it for 50 or 60 years that you begin to reflect and begin to understand it - appreciate the irony of it. I suppose that's the only way we can get a true perspective. We must take the event, add the rewards, subtract the consequences, wash it through a sieve then see what we are left with - dirt or gold.

If we find dirt we usually are pretty harsh on ourselves and others thinking there has to be someone to blame for the dirt. But if we have struck gold, we pat ourselves on the back then run around and tell everyone what a "Great job!" we did. Like we did it all by ourselves and now we are "genius material".

But really the joke's on us. You see I am thinking maybe we still reflect too early. That it is only seeing it from the far end, the backside, we can measure the true affect we have had on others and the world around us. And maybe, just maybe we shouldn't have been so harsh on that *"dirt thing"*.

Whether we know it or believe it - we all have a divine purpose. We were born with our purpose, our reason for being here. This purpose drives our decisions and our choices. Now if we are conscious of our purpose then we can make good choices. Those good decisions which line up with this purpose and then our life has infinite possibilities. These infinite possibilities lead us to feel fulfilled, energized and overflowing with love, kindness and the willingness to share all we have.

On the other hand, if we don't know our purpose we will think we are here on planet earth just to; hurry up and be sixteen to drive a car, hurry up and be twenty-one so we can drink, hurry up and be "older" so we can cohabitate and together accumulate as much stuff as possible - then hurry up and retire so we can sit on our stuff. If this is us, then we have missed our purpose *and our possibilities.* We have led a life - randomly making choices and decisions *that became our life.* And in the end as we take that last breath, it will hit us - our life was a mistake.

We were living someone else's life!

I don't want to end up like that. Do you?

Find your purpose and live true to it. You may find love, joy, truth and peace of mind where you least expect it. You may find so much that you have to give it away and when you do you'll get even more. It's like bread. Let's imagine your purpose is making bread. So you find the perfect recipe and follow the instructions precisely. You mix in the correct ingredients, knead the dough, shape it into a ball and let it breathe giving it time to rise. You will have to punch it down a time or two until it has risen fully and ready to be placed in the pan and baked at just the right temperature for the specified time. Remembering not to open that oven door and peek, "cause it could end up deflated" – flat bread, but not by choice! When the timer goes off and you open up that oven door all you'll be able to smell is the delicious aroma of perfectly baked bread. It looks so beautiful and tastes so good you will want to share it with everyone.

But, what would happen if you left out the yeast?

You'd have a brick!

You couldn't eat it and you couldn't use it as a door stop because it would get moldy. It is useless and you might as well throw it away and start all over again. There would be nothing to live on or to share with others. Without yeast nothing rises. Being in spirit is like that yeast. God, our source, who we emanate from, *is* the yeast *and* the key ingredient without which there is no bread. There is no bread of life and there is no "life in purpose".

Think about it.

There is energy in everything. We are walking flesh-suits of energy. Now we can walk around in these flesh-suits until the flesh wears out and the energy just dissipates somewhere. Or, we can add the yeast and when we do there is a chemical reaction, everything starts to bubble, to snap, crackle and pop! More energy is formed in the rising. We have multiplied our energy and created more. There's more for us to be joyous about. There's more to be fulfilled about and more to give and share with others. We have created an abundant life in spirit and one perfectly in line with our purpose.

And where there is abundance - *great things happen!* There is no fear. There is only satisfaction - satisfied in mind, body, soul and spirit.

This book has the yeast – it has been written fearlessly and is full of snap, crackle and pop! It has been beaten down a time or two, survived and baked at high heat (purposefully) - and now is ready to share. Like many of us, it is divided into several distinct parts, three in fact:

1. **_Discovery_** - *the awakening and searching after a crisis.*

My search and discovery; the "fight back" from a slow death that had been killing me one day at a time – for a long time.

2. **_Transformation_** - *the "remembering" and reflecting on life.*

My discovery shed light on the fact that the "who I had become" was a long way from the "who" I used to be and the "who" *I was meant to be.* It also made me realize I was not alone in my dilemma and if I could figure out what went wrong, then pay it forward, others too – could be set free. Or better still, they would not have to travel the road I had.

3) **_Inspiration_** – *the fruit of the vine.*

Some may think that inspiration comes before transformation. I suppose quite often that is the case. All I know that in my life, in the road from innocent to advocate - from naivety to twenty years of coaching, mentoring, founding and directing a successful program for those with life-controlling problems - *"I did it my way".*

One person told me after reading the beginning of this book that it was like "living in a constant stream of consciousness". Another said she got this visual image of me – crashing down an icy slope, out of control and on a shiny, silver metal sled shaped like a saucer.

Whew! "And that's exactly how it felt to me too!"

Others coined it honest and at times sounding like a stand-up comic routine, littered with descriptions so believable that they could actually see and feel it for themselves. I do hope the latter is true – because I want you to experience the roller-coaster ride "from here to there and back again" with me.

Several said they were confused – well, join the club buddy, me too!

And one brave soul out-right said "I didn't like it!"

She obviously was not an amusement-park person. And that's okay. Because you see, it evoked emotion. It connected with everyone differently, meaning each one was drawing on their own life experiences as they read it. P-e-r-f-e-c-t!

So... as you share this journey along side me, I hope your ideas and possibilities will begin to circulate and percolate. It has taken me almost a lifetime to figure some of these things out. I know you will be a much quicker study then I have been!

"I must be willing to give up what I am, in order to become what I will be."

- Albert Einstein

Good luck!

CHAPTER ONE

"So..."

The Crisis

"Get busy living or get busy dying."

This reflective quote from the movie, "The Shawshank Redemption" describes the place where I found myself upon awakening the morning after my fight or flight, near death experience three years ago. It also found me huddled on the hardwood floor of my office clutching my little dog, Tillie and my purse – the only two things I was able to grab as I escaped the house the night before.

"So, who are you, Susan?

You can't be good for anyone unless you know who you are first.

So, who am I? Who is this person?"

An involuntary shiver ran through me as I opened one eye and then the other. My bones felt cold and stiff from sleeping on the hard wood floor. Sleeping? Did I sleep at all or was it just a series of flashbacks then passing out from weariness, only to be startled awake again?

"Did it really happen?

What was I going to do next? What should I do next?"

Tillie's little body was still trembling and her front paws remained clenched tight around my arm. I closed my eyes again...

Breaking glass – that's the first thing I heard, then shattered glass everywhere.

There was no where to run!

Hot breath against my face, something sharp at my neck, "I should kill you, I'm gonna kill you..."

I felt paralyzed. He ranted and raved some more.

Should I say something? Should I try to move? These thoughts shot through my head.

How much time do I have? Am I going to die? Is this how my life is going to end? Am I ready?

From somewhere down deep inside me I felt a voice say, "Don't move." Then a stillness came over me as I began to melt into the mattress – deeper and deeper. I heard another voice, my voice repeating over and over "Jesus, Jesus, Jesus..."

I don't know how many times I said it or how long I lay there, it was as if time was suspended, floating above me.

Then I heard crashing as drawers where ripped out, thrown against the wall and hit the floor. There was another noise, faint in the distance. I don't know if it was a siren or the whine of a train whistle or what - but suddenly, I was alone.

A car door slammed and then nothing. I was afraid to move. I just laid there, seconds I suppose, but it felt like hours - until I felt the shivering. The shivering wouldn't stop. Then I realized little Tillie had tried to squeeze herself between me and the pillow, trying to hide and she was shivering, too.

The intruder was gone.

"But what if he comes back?"

The thought of it jolted me upright. *"I have to get out of here."*

I grabbed Tillie and tried to walk between the slivers of glass. Blood everywhere... Was it mine or his?

I ran down the stairs and found my purse hiding under a pile of papers. "Thank God, my car keys were still there!"

"Run!"

That's all I could think to do and so I did. Shoving Tillie in the car, I started the engine and sped as fast as I could down the street. I don't' remember what happened next or how long I drove but when I stopped the car I was parked in front of my office building. I fumbled to find the light switch, unlocked my office door, then bolted Tillie and myself in. I leaned against the door, limp. The room began spinning again.

What now?

"Just make it go away. Please make it go away!"

Three days later found the intruder behind bars, me back home cleaning up the mess and new locks on the doors. I made a list of all the things I had to do to feel safe and began to do them. But would I ever feel safe again?

I had to. I just had to!

Then it started. I don't now how to describe it but it felt as if there were two people inside my body fighting each other, trying to find their way out.

Was I going crazy?

I didn't know what to do. I was functioning – going to work then coming home and taking care of Tillie, protecting my home. But anytime when my mind wasn't busy on something constructive a terrifying feeling of being torn to pieces, my flesh being ripped from my body and nailed to the wall came over me. Then there were the flashes of light shooting out of my body like lasers. I couldn't breathe...

Was I trying to protect myself or was I trying to shed an overwhelming heaviness that felt like a lead blanket covering me as I lay in a tightly-closed coffin? I didn't know.

"Who are you?"

It again came from down somewhere deep. Deeper then I had ever felt anything before.

"Do something about it."

I don't know how long I sat there that day. But in the days to come, past images and random thoughts flooded my mind. They became my best friends.

And then one day I just knew. I *did* need to do something about it.

I didn't realize at the time what the something would be, what it would do or where it would take me. I just sat down at the computer and began to type.

It wasn't typing to escape – *it was typing to live, live again...*

The Transformation

Who am I?

Well, I've been a daughter, a mother, a wife, an employee, an employer, a friend, an owner, a renter, a winner and a loser – but I don't have a clue of *who* I am. I have been sad, scared, stressed, worried, guilty, depressed, suicidal, mad as hell, proud, confident, afraid and in love – but I don't think I have ever really been happy.

I can remember being as young as six years old and walking across the bridge in my home town with the Mahoning River rushing beneath me and being afraid. Afraid that I was going to fall or was it afraid I was going to jump? I don't know. Walking so fast over that bridge and being so out of breath, *and scared*! But I didn't fall. And I didn't jump!

I can remember my wedding day, being 20 years old and not knowing why I was marrying my soon-to-be-husband. Everyone else was getting married. It was the thing to do, all our friends were doing it. I don't think I loved him. I liked him, I liked him a lot - but I hardly smiled in any of the pictures. So I got married. But what I really wanted to do is go away to college and become an architect, unfortunately my parents said, "No!" So I said, "I'll get married". What was I thinking?

For years I lived in my head, in my thoughts and my daydreams. They were more real to me than my actual life. The day-to-day stuff I was just walking through – like a mechanical robot. Physically I was doing things like talking and working, but with no feelings. I was detached. Even now, I can remember the activities and the people but there's no emotion connected to them. It's as if the emotions were blotted out as the scene from a movie reel was slowing rolling along.

I was there, I see me but I can't feel me or anything else, anyone else...

The best thing about that time was the birth of my daughter. We did many things together - fun things, I know that. But I had a hard time feeling them. Even when I was "having fun" there was a part of me that couldn't feel happy, I held back. I held myself back. It was like I was watching myself doing it, I could see my body moving and I could hear my voice speaking but it wasn't connected to me. I didn't feel anything. Nobody knew me, the real me. I wouldn't allow them to.

How could I? I, didn't even know the real me.

No joy, no peace, no happiness. About the only emotion I had then was anger. Boy, could I feel that! It was the only emotion I could express openly and freely. But it was a blind anger, a blinding anger – an unjustified anger.

I remember an incident just after I was married. My husband and I got into this huge argument. It was about money, it always was about money. He had done something and I was furious! We were screaming at each other and I walked into the kitchen, I was so mad I felt like throwing something or hitting someone. I was pacing around and around trying to find something to destroy and all I could think to do was to open the refrigerator door and then slam it shut real hard.

Now I am sure that would have been a good alternative to punching someone's lights out, except this refrigerator had those little cups that held eggs built into the door. So when I slammed the door all the eggs went flying! Two dozen - 24 raw eggs, all broken and oozing. Do you know what 24 raw eggs broken with all that yellow and white slime does to the inside of a refrigerator?

You guessed it, it gets all over everything and then turns hard and glue-like - really fast.

After that I really went crazy. I stormed into the bedroom and locked the door, after that I don't remember what happened. That's what the anger would do to me. It was like living in a blackout until I calmed down and the anger left me. My husband cleaned up the mess himself, it had to have taken him hours.

And it wasn't just being angry at others that unleashed this monster. I could be mad at me or mad at an "it" – and it would happen. Like the time I tried to make a cake from scratch and it fell, wouldn't rise – it was ruined. Again, I saw red. This "red anger" would literally come over me and I couldn't control it! I picked up two softened sticks of butter and threw them as hard as I could against the cupboard door. They slowly slid down the wooden door until they plopped onto the floor. This mess I did clean up myself. Boy, did that cupboard door stay shiny and greasy for a long, long time!

I acted as if there was nothing wrong. I was responsible and accountable. I attended the birthday parties, bought gifts, celebrated Christmas and gave thanks at Thanksgiving. My body went through the mechanics but it had nothing to do with my emotions or my soul. I guess I was like the walking dead, only just alive enough to fool everyone.

I would only tell people what I wanted them to know. But my inner dreams, desires and hopes were isolated from the human race. I don't know when this started. Maybe it was around the age of 13, after my Aunt Bertie died. Her death was devastating to me. I loved her so much - we did so many fun things together. She and my mom were really close, closer than just sisters. They were confidants. We only lived about a mile or so away from her and saw her almost every day. I would stay over her house and in the morning we'd wake up and she would make me crepes.

She was the one who took me to taste my first "fast food", McDonald's – when the sign said "hundreds" sold, not millions. When my dad got laid-off from work and was out day after day trying to find anything to pay the bills and my mom had to go back to work, she was the one who took care of me. She taught me how to darn socks (that's back when you just didn't throw things away – you fixed them).

So, when she died - something died in me. And worse, something died in my mom. She was never the same. And so, it was like two people died, or maybe three. Life was never the same. I don't know if that is when I unconsciously decided to never let people in or trust enough to be vulnerable. Looking back now it does seem to makes sense.

I believe the first time I had a true emotion which I fully acted on was when my husband cheated on me with his old girlfriend, his high school sweetheart, and I plotted my revenge.

Revenge!

It consumed me! I calculated how I would get him back, make him jump through hoops of repentance, lull him into a false sense of security, have my own affair and then one day – dump him. Dump him hard. Let him feel the pain, let him feel the humiliation, let him feel the abandonment.

And I did. I did all that. I did it exactly like I said I would. Later to find out, the joke was on me. I didn't feel better or "normal". It just left me hollow inside and desperate to fill that void, that big black hole where my heart should have been. It also hurt all the people around me, innocent people. I don't recommend revenge as a solution.

So, for the next 20 years or so I drifted, drifted in and out my life...

So now, who am I?

I feel very lonely on Christmas Day and Christmas Eve. I miss my parents. I miss Ohio at Easter, Easter pie and Easter bread. I think it's the tradition. It means home to me, I guess it always will. I took all of this for granted of course. That is the curse of being young. You think the good things will last forever. Or maybe it's just that you don't realize what the good things really are. Not until you don't have them anymore. It's only then that you have to dig real deep, reach inside and remember what is important. *Fight for what is important!*

I like the beach, the breeze and salt air blowing in my face. I like getting up before the sun rises and walking on the beach, watching the colors explode and taking photographs of the gorgeous sun rises. I can think at the beach. I get insight and ideas at the beach. And I can relax at the beach - it must be the ocean. The tide takes the water out to sea, maybe to cleanse it or maybe to pick up some valuables. Then it brings it back to shore depositing beautiful shells and starfish. That's the feeling I get when I am at the beach. It's like my old thoughts and worries are drawn out of me and waves of peace and calm crash over me. It calms my spirit. Maybe it's because it helps me connect with my spirit.

Maybe *that's* my way of connecting...

I love to take pictures of the sky and clouds. I love how the sky looks before a storm when it is dark and ominous - scary. I love the wind when it whistles through the trees and you can see the flip side of the leaves flapping and swaying as the sky gets darker and darker. I love the thunder and the lightening, too. And the feeling of electricity right before it starts to rain. I love to breathe that air in and close my eyes and feel...

I love people watching. I love to drive my car fast with the windows down and the music playing *loud* - the 60's and 70's, of course. Is there any other music?

I love dogs. I love my dog, Tillie. She is exactly like her name sounds, it fits her personality perfectly. She is a tiny airheaded genius. She goes through life at one speed "full force ahead". She lives to play and if she's not playing she's sleeping, so she can play some more. And she doesn't need anyone or anything to play with. She plays with the air, the couch, toilet paper, leaves, my underwear and any scrap of paper she can find. But the best is when she plays games with herself. She'll stand at the top of the stairs with a tennis ball in her mouth and throw (yes, I did say throw) it down the stairs and then race to try to get to the bottom of the steps before the ball does.

She loves to be in control and be in charge. So she lines all her toys up in a row, there's; teddy bear, yellow M&M candy, Santa Claus, tiny teddy bear holding a heart, baby rabbit, big kangaroo rabbit, tennis ball, Snoopy, squeaky rubber ice cream cone and yellow, door-stopper dog. Then she sits on her pillow and looks down on her subjects and barks orders at them. Queen Tillie. Living life to the fullest! All that's missing is a crown.

I am not a painter but I would love to learn to paint. And I want to learn a foreign language. I would love to feel healthier and lose some weight. I think I have lived my whole life in a state of losing weight. I've gauged my life according to the number on the scale and the dress size in my closet.

I would love to spend more time with my daughter, Stacey, talk and do things together. Find out who she is. *I know she already knows*!

I need to feel free. To have a feeling of freedom and "carefree-ness"!

But today, I am tired, tired of making people happy, fixing things, cooking, being told what to do and what I can't do, worrying about money, having no money, not having any fun, not able to buy anything and not really knowing what I want. But mostly I am tired of being tired. I am tired of being in pain and not able to physically do the things I need to do and want to do. Is this what despair feels like?

After both my parents died I felt like I didn't belong to anyone, that there wasn't anyone left who knew me as a baby, child, or teenager. There was no one who loved me unconditionally. I really was lost. I yearned for the past. I felt so alone, abandoned. Being an only child and in an isolated marriage left me drifting, stranded out at sea. Eventually most of those feelings went away but there are times when I still miss the place where I grew up. I want to relive all those memories. *Depths of despair, again - abandoned.*

Recently I read the book "Proof of Heaven" by Dr. Eben Alexander – it is wonderful! His revelations after his near-death experience are insightful and life-changing. Here's one that especially spoke to me:

"On a basic level, we all feel (wrongly) like orphans, given away. Without recovering the memory of our larger connectedness and unconditional love of our Creator – we will always feel lost here on earth. Maybe that is why so many struggle with life here on earth."

Breathe...

I love the smell of freshly cut grass, roses and my puppy after she's had a bath. I love fresh flowers in the house, pedicures and massages. I love to listen to music and fall asleep in the chair. I love to window shop, randomly looking through the stores touching everything, especially the stuff that says **"Don't touch"**. No schedules, no problems to solve and no questions to answer. It's been so long since I have been able to think, really think. Ponder the possibilities. Investigate ideas. Question the status quo.

Today, is it all just about "surviving"? Or must we plan to live - and then live?

I realize that for all of us it's important to BE ALIVE until the day we die. We must act alive, to participate in one's own life, to make a life, to continue to create. It's not a waste or being selfish. In fact, it's okay to be selfish!

Know yourself - *it's the most unselfish thing you can do*! Otherwise, you aren't living - you are just existing. I have lived too many years just existing, trying to dot all the "i's" and cross all the "t's". It's important to have morale character and be ethical, but that has to be the under girth of it all because *living* is the activity.

Living life is the activity! The others are the nouns, the results - what your life shows.

So, now I guess I am a philosopher. I love the movie "My Blue Heaven" with Steve Martin because "how" his character lived his life, *was* his philosophy. What he believed was his truth – his philosophy. And his philosophy changed the people around him.

Great! Now what, a bucket list?

I'd like to throw a bucket. Really hard!

Okay what's gonna go in my bucket, hmm...

Well, I want to write a book (oops, I guess I am doing that one), fly a plane, travel to Rome and see the Sistine Chapel, go to the Kentucky Derby and wear an outrageous hat and drink a mint julep. I want to go to a fancy "spa" and have massages, facials and long quiet walks barefoot. I want to take philosophy and ethics classes, I love the debate. I want to take painting classes and I want to go to Monte Carlo, hobnob with rich people, gamble and win! Ha, ha, ha! I want to be eccentric, make business cards, put out a shingle and go into the business of telling other people what to do. I think I would be pretty good at that!

I want to be humorous, but maybe I am already that. Most days I think I am just here on planet earth for comic relief. I want to laugh, really laugh. Just be silly, not worry about what others think and just laugh. I want to go to Hawaii and explore volcanoes. I want to drive along the coast of California - Malibu, I think. It sounds so posh. In a bright red convertible with the wind blowing my hair, looking down and seeing the Pacific Ocean and the waves crashing on the rocks.

I find it amazing that my thoughts flit like a butterfly from flower to flower and my mood fluctuates at the slightest whim. Ideas are coming and they are interesting and creative not boring and stiff or obligated like my life has been.

Think of it, everyday you wake up and the day is a clean slate. Oh, sure, there is yesterday's stuff to deal with. *But you are dealing with a 24 hours that has never been and never will be again.* In fact, the time it took me to write this sentence is gone. I can't repeat it or get it back. That part of my life is over, it's the past. I can't change it.

That's why most people don't realize you can't change the past. So why keep living something over and over that you can't change? Do things today that you won't have to waste your time fixing tomorrow. So you will have the time to plan for the spontaneous.

Hey, that can be my philosophy; "Plan for the spontaneous". See the contraction?

No, *be* the contradiction.

I want my life to be exciting. But it must be the good exciting. Not the bad exciting like escaping from your house - shattered glass and shattered life everywhere, from a madman at 1 am with only your purse and your dog clutched under your arm. That's bad exciting.

But wasn't it this bad exciting that began my search and discovery?

Hmmm... Sometimes you just can't explain life.

So, if I am going to tell others what to do I must be very wise, why else would anyone want to hear what I had to say? So, what do I know? Let me think. Well, first I think I need to separate what I *know* to be *true* from what I know. Big difference there...

I know I was born and someday I will die. That one is a little bit too easy. No one will listen to me say that one. How about:

I know that I am the only person who can make me happy. And choosing happy is a choice that I have to make every day. But do I choose to be happy or do I choose to let people or circumstances interfere with my happiness?

I think my natural tendency, my nature, is to let things happen to me. Not to question but to accept things at face value. Accept what people are telling me. It takes work on my part to be attentive, inquisitive and sociable. I would rather just stroll along the beach or in the woods soaking up the wonders around me. So, making friends, getting involved in hobbies and exploring the world does not come natural to me. I have to be purposeful and intentional in doing these things.

So, how do I make the jump and go from not liking the effort it takes to do these things to - *l-o-v-i-n-g it?*

I don't know.

As an only child I spent time either by myself or with adults. I was more of an observer of people, a studier, you might say of human beings. I have always been very content to be alone and spend time with myself. I guess that added to the "living in my head" thing. This poem just about sums it all up for me:

How Long?

In my head I am a princess,
In my dreams I am powerful and smart.
In my sleep I am courageous,
That's where I live - in my head.

There I can do all things,
My ideas never fail.

People never let me down,
I, never let me down.

The life there is exciting!
Fun lasts and there is no work to be done.
I can float from roof top to roof top,
Unimpeded and free.
Maybe it's the free I need,
The free I long for.
How long must I wait?
How long?

> \- Susan Farah

Sorry, I digressed a little. Where was I?

Oh yes, choosing to be happy.

Choosing, not to be negative, stressed or aggravated. It's hard work, you know. Learning to identify when it's starting to happen and intentionally stopping and saying, "Nope, I am not going to let that upset me." Then moving on, be positive and getting back on that "perfection train".

Hey, that's what I can call it - my perfection train going to Hawaii. It's similar to that song, "Midnight Train to Georgia," but just not famous.

So, some days my perfection train is speeding down the track going 100 miles an hour and sometimes it is stuck at a railroad crossing, going back and forth with the crossing lights flashing and the gates down.

I wonder if everyone feels like this or am I the only one?

Back to choosing, I bet you guessed I have just read a book on the Law of Attraction. Well, actually I listened to it, you gotta love audio books. I don't know who invented them but that person is a genius! Hope they copyrighted it and made a lot of money. Think of it, driving your car while knowledge is being sucked up into your brain like a sponge, amazing.

You know what else? You can talk to this book as it is playing, too. And you must because you're agreeing with it or saying, "Wow, that's me!" So, you're talking and shaking your head and having a good ole time in your car not realizing people are looking at you and thinking you're "nuts!"

So, back to this Law of Attraction which says I can have what I want.

Well, I like that because I am beginning to know what I want and I want to have feelings about what I want. It also says I am what I believe I am and that what I think and believe is powerful and will dictate my life. Now this is a really good thing because *I want the control over me*, not someone else having the control over me.

I have gone too long and spent too much time believing that others or "life" had control over me and that I couldn't change things. I *am tenacious* and now that I have a hold of this "attracting" good instead of "attracting" bad thing, I am not going to let that sucker go. I am going ride it till it keels over.

So, all aboard! Look out!

"The perfection train has left the station!"

CHAPTER TWO

"So What..."

So, I was driving along in my car this morning on my way to work trying to put this new philosophy into action. It was a beautiful morning; blue sky, sunny, in the 70's, a slight breeze and no humidity – perfect. I was thinking of all the "happy songs" that make me smile: "It's a Beautiful Morning", "I Feel Pretty" (remember Jack Nicholson singing that in Anger Management?), "Just a Spoonful of Sugar Makes the Medicine Go Down" (love that Mary Poppins), and I'm a Believer (The Monkees – you have to smile at that one). I sang each one out loud and felt pleasantly charged-up and soon began dancing in my seat.

My mind was concentrating hard trying to remember more happy songs as I whizzed by an open yellow and white striped umbrella lying along the side of the road.

"Ah ha!" I thought.

Then it came to me, a happy song "Singing in the Rain". And I began singing, "I'm singing in the rain, just singing in the rain", when suddenly I stopped. It hit me all at once – **happy** - *happy frequency, singing happy songs, searching for more happy songs, see umbrella, happy song ("Singing in the Rain") pops into brain, sang happy song* = **HAPPY.**

It worked!

I really am a big transmitter and magnet. The umbrella was drawn into my field of vision, which in turn, released the memory of the happy song I was searching for out of the archives of my mind. I laughed all the way to work.

I laughed at work and sang and whistled. And when several things happened to me that last week would have ruined my day and had me mumbling, grumbling and stressed, I *intentionally* said out loud, "No Way!" I just let it go and moved on to my next task. I had five great days in a row, that's never happened!

It was perfect. Two staff members even resigned and, guess what? It was okay.

Well, I had to try something else to see if this was really working and not just a fluke. So I put the fleece out there. Lets try the financial abundance, the "more than enough", the "plenty" frequency. Ask, believe and receive. I like round numbers and $100,000.00 sounded like a really *great round number* to me. So that's what I asked for and that everyday I would receive a monetary blessing which would work towards that $100,000.00. (Don't worry, later I found out this was the beginning of a spiritual journey – not a financially lucrative one).

The next day I received a $50 gift card in the mail, a rebate from the new phone I just bought. It was expected but unexpectedly, it came within a few days. The next day I was doing my back-stretching exercises on the floor of my living room. While I was down there I glanced over my shoulder and something caught my eye. I reached my hand under the couch and there it was - a crumpled-up $5.00 bill.

Wow! Two days in a row.

The following day I found out that new tags for my car were only going to cost me $28. I thought it would be at least $50, saving money counts too! The day after that, I was quoted $394.00 for four brand new tires. But when the lady rang up the bill she said, "It will be $364.00." Again, I saved money, this time $30. I can't wait to see what comes my way tomorrow!

I could really get into this "being a giant magnet thing". I definitely want to be attracting doe-ra-me or is that dough-ray-me?

I believe a very important part of this new found phenomenon is that we need to be *looking* for those blessings - being intentional, otherwise we miss them. They are there for you and I, *but we will not see them if we aren't looking for them.*

Keeping in the spirit, I came up with a snappy, little acronym for H-A-P-P-Y:

H - *Harmonious* **A** - *Awesome* **P** - *Positive* **P** - *Perfect* **Y** - *Yippee!*

So I went around all day at work telling everyone my "HAPPY" and they just laughed. S. said to me, "You sound like Gary Busey, he does that all the time with words."

I thought, "Great!" I am not sure that was the comparison I was looking for. But, no worries...I can make fun of myself as good as the next guy!

So, I've been a Presbyterian, a Catholic, a born-again Christian, a democrat and a republican. That covers religion and politics. I've been a believer in causes and a skeptic. I've been skinny and fat, a blonde and a brunette, a Yankee and a Southerner, short and getting shorter, young and now definitely getting "older".

I've been liberal and conservative. I've marched and I've sat. And through it all I've tried to make sense of my life. The truth is, the only thing I have come up with so far is that everything I've experienced (especially the bad) prepared me for the next thing that came along in my life. And it seems that every time I have been critical or judgmental, Wham! There came that exact life experience for me to live out.

And guess what?

Now I understand and have decided - I definitely don't want to be judgmental anymore. So, after being depressed, falling in love with someone who had addictions and being in an abusive situation (all of which I had been judgmental about), the light bulb finally went off. It illuminated me to the fact that I am tired of life's lessons and I am ready now to take a break from learning. I mean the good news was that those experiences led me to starting a 501c3 non-profit and working with women with life-controlling problems for ten years. But now I am ready for peace and hoping for a little tranquility!

So, what else do I like?

Honestly, I am starting to like me again. I forgot I used to like me. I forgot there was a lot to like. It's funny, how something like that can be stripped away from you, piece by piece, a little at a time over the years until you are just an empty shell. But amazingly enough you can just turn that dial, change that channel and get a new frequency! And that big ole transmitter magnet you are comes alive and, all of a sudden, new things are sticking to you. Like a big Hoover or Electrolux vacuum cleaner - you are sucking stuff up. Well, I've decided the only stuff I want to suck up for a while is money and happiness.

Happy – Yippee!

I like to watch old episodes of "Leave It to Beaver" and "The Brady Bunch". I like learning. In fact, now that my brain is defogging and I can think again I realize that I love learning. I would love to go back to college and finish my degree. They say you are never too old - I don't know about that. Because I have a hard time retaining new information now. It just seems to fall out of my brain. I just can't read a book. I keep reading the same page over and over again and can't remember what I just read.

So, I thought "this is ridiculous!" There must be a trick I can do to fix that problem.

So, I got a book on CD (audio-book) and listened to it in my car. That really helped but it's hard to always find the books you want on CD. There was a book on "intention" by Dr. Wayne Dyer I really wanted to read. I was like, "Oh no, I am going to waste my money again and it will just sit and collect dust on my shelf again." But then that magnet thing starting working and an idea popped into my head.

Make it audio. *Read it out loud to yourself!*

I don't have the most exciting voice but here I am reading this book out loud to myself and you know, darn it, it's working! I can remember some of what I am reading or is that "what I am hearing?" Ha, ha, ha!

Oops, I just thought of something else I want to put on my bucket list or in the bucket, whichever. I want to be a conversationalist. I envy people who can make small talk. You know those people who just start chattering away and never stop. They are the ones that can start up a conversation with anyone about anything and keep it going, forever. Not me, I struggle to think of talking about the weather. And everyone knows if you have to talk about the weather *you have nothing to say*! How boring.

Oh yes, I want to be interesting too, another drop in my bucket. A while back I had been seeing a therapist and one day I walked into her office and she said, "Oh, I am so glad it's you. I thought I was seeing someone else today. But I love when you come, you are so i-n-t-e-r-e-s-t-in-g!"

She did say it just like that with the dashes and the "i-n-t-e-r-e-s-t-i-n-g" stretching out l - o - n - g. I wonder, when your therapist thinks you're interesting – *is that a good thing or a bad thing?*

I wish I could invent something like the paper clip or sticky notes. I love those sticky notes. I'd be rich!

Who would of thought it - that folding a little piece of wire could make you a billionaire? Fascinating... a paper clip... Just think of how many paper clips have been sold over the years. Why can't I think of something like that?

I wonder, does everyone think like this?

I think I am going to add that to my bucket list. I want to invent something. I mean I don't need to invent something important like penicillin or a great mathematical theory. I don't need to win the Nobel Prize, just a little something that will make me rich beyond my wildest dreams.

So, I love to shoe shop and for purses, too. The older I get the more I like shoes and purses. What's up with that? My mother's favorite thing was to shop for shoes and purses. In fact, whenever she and my dad had a fight she would buy a new pair of shoes or a purse. I've talked to some other women in their 50's and they have said this same phenomenon is happening to them, too. That is weird. I am turning into my mother. Pretty soon (since I am shrinking,) I'll be 4"10, have a 100 pairs of shoes in my closet that I don't wear and hand out pieces of chocolate to everyone. Just call me Dottie.

It's late and I am getting silly. "Good night, don't let the bedbugs bite!"

I'm still awake...

Still awake...

Hey, I was thinking. This is like something from nothing. So, what I am doing *right now* is inventing. So, *I am* an inventor! Wow!

It reminds me of the movie, "What About Bob?" I love that movie. I can't figure out who is the funniest; phobic Bob, his psychiatrist who needs a psychiatrist, or the psychiatrist's naive wife who keeps saying "What about Bob?" But, after Bob conquers something that he thinks he can't, he always states the obvious. For example, he went sailing and then stated, "I'm a sailor!"

So guess what? "I am an inventor!" "I am a writer".

Who knew?

And now, it's good night...

CHAPTER THREE

"So okay..."

So, I am about 30 days into my new journey, my rite of passage. How do you think I am doing?

Really? Hmmm...

So, I have been a negotiator, a mentor, a rescuer, an enabler, a problem-solver and an idea maker-upper. And, I not only talk to myself but answer myself back. How else can I possibly get the right answer? I like to read between the lines. You know, try to figure out what is really going on.

I think I have spent my whole life analyzing other people and I don't have a clue about myself. Who the heck am I? What do I want? Where am I going? And most importantly, what's it all about? So, I've started to play a game with myself. It's called, "If I had a name like that".

One day a guy called our house and when I answered the phone he said, "Hello, my name is Tommy Donuts". Do you believe it, Tommy Donuts! With a name like that I imagine Tommy is about 5'7" with a round face and a round body, weighing about 250 pounds and he loves donuts. With a name like that I would have to change it to Tommy Cream-Stick. This way he could still love donuts but at least he would be tall.

Speaking of tall, I always wanted to be tall. I remember telling someone, "I wish I was tall - like 5'3". They cracked up! But I was serious. When you are 5'1" you *do* think 5'3" is tall. In school I was always in the front of the line. I was always first. I can't see anything during a parade and five pounds looks like fifteen on me because there is no where for the weight to go!

Billy Bob Thornton. Now who would of thought that "with a name like that" Billy Bob would turn out to be a successful actor, writer and have dated and married some of the most beautiful women in the world? And he's not that cute. No offense Billy Bob, but it's true. I think Billy can handle the truth, don't you? I mean he's rich and famous, for Pete's sake.

For Pete's sake, I wonder how we ever got started saying that? Was there really a Pete? And what did somebody do for his sake? And how about "okie dokie"? My parents said that a lot, so I bet it's been around for a long time. Was there an okie and a dokie? I mean okie is a little like okay so I can see that. But, dokie? That doesn't sound like anything. Well, maybe donkey but that doesn't make sense. Okay donkey?

Well now, maybe that does make sense. Maybe the originator was saying, "Okay you dumb ass." Hah!

Get the lead out, that's another one my dad used to say all the time. I wonder who started that one. My day would always say that when he wanted us to hurry up. So I guess it has to do with hurrying, going faster. Maybe, lead = ammunition, load your gun and shoot and do it in a hurry or someone is going to shoot you!

My dad was a hunter and he loved the TV show "The Rifleman". In fact, he had business cards made up with "Have Truck Will Travel" on it (he was a carpenter, one of his many talents), just like the Rifleman's motto – "Have Gun Will Travel". Those are some good memories, the good old days.

How about "cat's got your tongue?" How could a cat get your tongue? And, if he could, what would he do with it? Could you see a little cat head and this little cat heads' mouth opens up and this big old tongue comes flying out. It probably couldn't even fit in there in the first place! And what if he tried to give it back? There would be cat hair and fur balls all over it!

I wouldn't put that tongue in my mouth!

Do cats really have nine lives? Why do they get more than one? Are they special or do they just do so many dumb things that God said, "I better give them nine because they're going to need them." I have trouble dealing with one life I sure wouldn't want nine!

Can you imagine it? When you just about get your life figured out a little bit, Wham! Start over. Of course, it could be a do-over. You remember do-over's when you were a kid. You made a mistake or gave the wrong answer and you yelled "Do-over!" If you were lucky the other person would let you have another chance. Maybe that's what cats get, more chances.

So, now a couple of days have passed and it's been good but I feel all jammed up. Thoughts about the past have taken residence in my brain, rent-free. Even listening to old Simon and Garfunkel songs and singing along real loud didn't help, except for "Feeling Groovy". I had forgotten they wrote that song. I did laugh at that one; remembering saying "groovy", giving the peace sign, mini skirts and the never to be forgotten "flower power". I was very opinionated then. I thought I knew it all and I was going to fight for it. You know - women's lib, and all that.

I remember I was working at Dollar Bank and pregnant, my boss's wife was pregnant too. And he used to share some funny stories with me. I don't remember exactly what happened but something did and I was furious about it. I stormed into his office and told him off and stormed out, slamming the door behind me really hard. It had something to do with my women's lib slant on a situation. I was sitting at my desk fuming when he came over and said, "It's all right, Susan, my wife's pregnant too."

What?!

Your wife's pregnant too?

You think this is a hormonal thing?

Now my hair was on fire! How patronizing! I didn't talk to him for days.

Looking back, it *was* hormonal and so non-important that I can't even remember what it was. But I do remember the fool I made of myself. Oh well, c'est la vie. That's what getting older does for you, makes you less stupid.

And my boss, well he and three of his cohorts, the other loan officers, used to recite "word for word" The Wizard of Oz. They literally could recite every word of it. The four of them played all the parts and would sit there for hours doing it, usually while they were supposed to be working. Us little secretaries (we were secretaries then not Administrative Assistants), would be typing away listening to our Dictaphones, and transcribing. Does anyone remember what a Dictaphone is?

The boys would be singing, "Lions and Tigers and Bears, Oh My!" My boss was the funniest. He was tall, about 6'2", weighed nothing and looked like a string-bean. In fact, that was the nickname we made up for him. He didn't know that of course. Slick was another one of the officers. He was very proper and combed his hair straight back using a lot of slick-um gel to hold it down, so Slick.

Their boss had a great nick name too. One, we had given him of course, Benny (after the Elton John song, "Benny and the Jets"). And then there was his secretary, "Donut". Donut would flirt with him every morning bringing him a donut, hence the nickname "Donut".

So, one of the loan officers was leaving and our department was throwing him a party at a fancy restaurant called The Mansion. Myself and three other secretaries decided we would be the entertainment for the evening and give him a roast. Well, as the story goes us four dressed in black hot pants, high heels, bunny ears and bunny tails. And not only did we roast the leaving comrade, we roasted everyone; String Bean, Slick, Benny and little Donut, too! We had one too many martinis waiting for our stage debut. It was a good thing that Benny and Donut had had too many martinis too, because somehow they didn't hear or realize we were making fun of them.

Score one for blackouts. We didn't need to lose our jobs.

Oh, then there was the Crazy String that we accidentally sprayed on the ceiling. It stayed there until the restaurant burned down a few years later. Hope it wasn't due to the Crazy String. Has anyone ever even heard of Crazy String? It's obsolete now.

And speaking of obsolete I can't believe what has become extinct in my lifetime. You know, like the dinosaurs did in the caveman's time.

Remember the movie "Michael" where John Travolta is this big, grubby angel? There is this scene where he is in the back seat of the station wagon singing, "All You Need Is Love" (The Beatles) and he finally gets everyone in the car to sing along. What a great scene and song. I have decided to simplify my life and down-size. The new theme song for my life will be, "All I Need Is Love – and Allergy Medicine". I really need my allergy medicine.

I just realized something that a friend of mine told me is really true. I use movies I've seen to describe situations and how I feel, <u>a lot</u>! It's like that's an easy way for me to connect with and relate to people. *That's not a bad thing, is it?*

Hey, it's like the scene from "Scrooged" when the main character is trying to convince the ghost from his past that he did wonderful things when in reality he had only lived through the TV shows he watched.

"You just did it again". *What?*

I said, "You did it again".

OMG, you are right and besides that I am holding a conversation with myself again, alone.

"How else are you going to get the right answer?"

Stop it!! Change the subject.

"Okay, I will".

I am listening to another audio book by Dr. Wayne Dyer, called "Inspiration" "How to Live an Inspired Life". About how we need to take each day and every moment in it and make it count. Look for opportunities to help others *and* to realize when help has been sent to us in the form of a person, thought or object.

Pretty heavy stuff...I really like it though. I like the idea that life is just not there and "that's all there is". There has to be a reason we are here. A reason *I* am here. Not just to pay taxes and die.

So, my normal personality is to be nice. But I do tend to be so preoccupied with my thoughts and so intent on the task that I am doing, that I don't pay attention to the people around me. I can really do a good job of ignoring people. Well, Dr. Dyer would not be pleased with this.

As a result, I have begun to make it a point to TALK TO PEOPLE!

It is not easy. It goes against my very nature. But since one of my bucket items is to become a conversationalist, it's probably very good practice for me. I am getting a little better at it. And some days it is actually fun.

But tell me, do you ever feel like this?

My Secret

I have a secret,
No one knows.
You can't guess it,
It's just for me to know.
Should I share it?
But if I do,
It won't be secret anymore.
One for good, two for bad,
How many should I bet down for sad?
It's a shame you don't see,
Without this secret
I really could be me!

                              - Susan Farah

CHAPTER FOUR

"So great…"

Or as I like to put it, you are not growing older you are just navigating life through the social network.

Typewriters, you can't find them anymore. I remember zooming away on my electric typewriter care-free and content. And then BOOM! It died on me. Tragedy! I had to finish the grant I was writing, and quickly. I rushed to Walmarts, Office Max and a few other places and was shaken into an appalled reality, "They don't make them anymore"!

What you say?

How can they not make typewriters? How can anyone type anything? The sales people laughed, shook their heads and got irritated with me. They thought I had just crawled out from under a rock. Computers, I got a rude awakening that no matter how much I didn't want to have to turn on, touch and use that "thing" there was no other way to type. Enter the age of Administrative Assistants, bye-bye secretaries. Good-bye yellow brick road and Donut - hello dealing with a "thing" that thought it was smarter than me but at any given time could shut down, blow up and lose all the hard work I had just done. Progress? Really?

So, speaking of obsolete, I was watching an infomercial yesterday about mini facelifts. Now for a number of years I have avoided full-length mirrors, getting my picture taken and bright lighting in bathrooms. My 40+++ diminishing eyesight had really been a team player in helping me accomplish this goal. But as I was watching this infomercial on "mini" facelifts I realized I had that neck. You know the neck that looks like Tom Turkey on Thanksgiving Day. Yup, that's the one.

OMG! How about that very odd and unattractive side view? And I had those deep lines protruding downward from the sides of my mouth. Heck! I looked worse than some of those women on the screen. I have always been against plastic surgery. You know, people are beautiful, this is the way God made us and aging is a natural part of the journey, blah, blah, blah....

Bologna! I look old! I don't want to. So, yes you know what I am going to say next - I called the number on the screen.

Now the job of the person on the other end of the phone is to sell. I know that. I am prepared just to listen and get information. I am not going to get caught up in romanticizing about looking 25 again. I am not going to let anyone talk me into anything. Well, ten minutes later I was making one of those "free" appointments for a consultation in a city four hours from where I live. Hey, I hate to go four blocks out of my way and will sit in a line of stopped cars for 20 minutes just to go two blocks less in my drive to work. So on June 11th I am going to have a doctor, I hope, tell me how my life can be improved by removing the wrinkles from my face.

Hey, I earned those wrinkles!

But you know, I'd rather just have the memories and let someone else have the wrinkles.

What really did it for me was when I went to the mirror (this is really a big no-no for someone over 55) and pulled the skin on the sides of my face up and back "just a little".

WOW! I remember that person.

That's the person I see in my head everyday. The one that is about 20 years younger and still optimistic. Isn't it funny how what we feel and look like in our head is different than what other people see. I want *that* person, hence, my facelift appointment on the 11th.

I don't know, should I lose the turkey skin? Gobble, gobble. Hmmm...

It's been about six weeks into my new life and I am beginning to see a few specks of the old me emerging. I am not dreading to take a shower. In fact, I actual enjoy the "being clean" rather than the disheveled look. I no longer crave anything sweet and don't have the urge to down a spoonful of granulated sugar (or brown sugar in a pinch), just to satisfy my ravenous appetite for it. In fact, now the raw carrots taste so sweet it's like eating a candy bar. Well, almost.

When I talk to myself now I'm not making myself more depressed but I'm making myself laugh. Yes, I can still laugh. I thought that one was gone forever. The affirmations, the positive inner talk, the meditating music, flowers inside and outside the house and eating practically no carbs has not only dropped about 15 pounds off my body but the wear and tear of the last fifteen years from my mentally and emotionally used and abused face, and my soul. It really is true. We are what we eat, think and believe.

So, I wonder if I can do that with the turkey-skin? What do you think?

I got the idea of trying to feng shui my life. I can't say this was a spiritual revelation. I got it from the movie "It's Complicated" and it sounded good, like it was a positive thing. And I am all about the positive now. Remember?

H-A-P-P-Y – harmonious, awesome, positive, perfect, yippee!

Well, since we are now in the 21st century the logical thing to do, yes just say it, "Look it up on the internet." Do you know how much information is there? I could spend the rest of my life learning about feng shui and be dead from having bad chi or **ban age,** something like that.

I really did try to figure it out. First you have to know the direction your house sits, what direction the rooms of your house face and very importantly, the front door. So here I am with a clipboard in my hand trying to figure out what is; S, N E, W, NE, NW, SE and SW. I think my front door is east. Now I must make sure nothing is blocking the flow of energy to and through the door and throughout the house. Okay, did it. Oops, staircase facing door; must counteract that problem. Okay, done.

Hmmm...

So, I spent a day walking around my house in and out, moving furniture, changing colors and moving knickknacks. Knickknacks are my collection of collectibles and antiques, that's what they call old stuff now – antiques. Maybe I'm an antique too. And darn it, wouldn't you know. I did feel better. It did look brighter and lighter. Cut, trimmed and edged the yard, yup - feel better. Cleaned out the closets, got rid of clutter. Yup, better.

You know, I think us humans have a feng shui thermometer already built into us. We just need to tap in to it. I do feel better when the yard looks nice and there are flowers around, space to walk between the furniture and my closets and drawers are neat.

It's like the spring cleaning my mom and every other woman used to do and make her daughter do back in the 50's and 60's. They just didn't call it feng shui, they called it housework. Dottie was "fen shui-ing" and didn't even know it!

Go mom! And all those other "Leave It to Beaver" moms, too!

Where was I? Oh, yeah.

I guess I have always known on some general level that we have several parts to us, and they are all interrelated. Mind – body – soul - spirit. I have spiritual beliefs that are very important to me. They steady me and help me maneuver through my life. But I have lived much of my life separated from this knowledge. Trying to be good and going to church when possible isn't what this is about. It's different than that, more than that. And that's becoming exciting to me now.

There is a freedom starting to rise up in me. I can feel it. Not all the time or everyday but I have real glimpses of feeling free. There is an authentic person, an authentic being inside me trying to get out, break out. Or maybe get back or break back in. I used to be this ball of energy with a purpose in life, but living-up to expectations, the rules and accumulating things got in the way of the essence of me. Well, I have spent the first 58 years of my life burying. Yes dumping the old dirt on that pure essence, so I guess I can take the next 58 digging myself out.

Did I tell you how great I am feeling? My memory has improved dramatically, too. I am grateful for my perfect self. In fact that is part of what I do each morning, my ritual. I talk to myself (nothing new) but what is new - is what I *say* to myself. Here goes:

"Thank you for my perfect brain, my perfect memory and the perfect electrical charges going off perfectly in my brain. Thank you for my perfect eyesight and my perfect hearing and so on."

I think you get the picture.

I spend about twenty minutes going through each part of my body and being grateful for the perfection of them. And lastly, I say thank you for my perfect well being because, I am perfect for the task of being me today. God made me that way. I was made perfectly, before I decided to throw a lifetime of unnecessary stuff at myself and let it get in the way of me. The *"me"* I was meant to be.

Like in the movie "Look Who's Talking" where Mikey says, '"Tell me about it, you spend nine months trying to get out and then a lifetime trying to get back in." Yeah, tell me about it.

In addition to the perfection talk, I am reading and reading. For so long my mind was trapped, like a bear in a bear trap. But now I want to learn new things and understand that I am not just this body aging by the second, and then one day will disintegrate. But I am connected to something, something eternal. The something that was before me and will continue after me. Something I will still be a part of.

And that "something else" I have learned is that I have always been creating my life, and I have to take responsibility for that. If I don't like what I have created then I am the one who needs to do something about it! I can't keep blaming other people if my life isn't what I want it to be. I have to reach back and remember who I am. Find my authentic self and create my life - me, no one else.

No one else is responsible for making me happy or sad. I can choose to be happy or I can choose to be sad. I can take each minute of every day and make it mean something or I can let it slip by and blame someone else.

That's empowerment! That's potential.

That is seeing what I want and living my life so *it is _my life_*. Then my life will mean something and stand for something bigger and greater than myself. It will be part of the vast collection of other humans who are doing the same. Who are changing lives - their own and other's.

"Who-rah!"

CHAPTER FIVE

"So What the Heck...?"

So, do you know what happened next? I blew it!

Things were going along so well. I was feeling great. I guess you could say I was on a pink cloud of my new self. Literally, I mean pink is my color. I believe pink is a power color, it is a fallacy that pink is for girls. Pink is empowerment, it is power! It is warm and perky and just makes you feel good, hence power.

When you feel good about yourself, you feel powerful, like nothing can touch you. You are in control and you are confident. That is just where I was, I was confident, relaxed and had the world on a string. It was going great.

Then, I blew it.

Well, I don't know if I blew it, sabotaged myself or I just slipped into old behavior. But the slow downhill slide started. It started with an interruption by way of an old feud. At first I held my ground, my newly-founded ground. But gradually I lost my focus. Negativity crept back into my life and into my vocabulary.

I was struggling again. I was feeling depressed and stressed. My brain felt foggy. I began to try to force the positive and perfection I had been feeling before. I wasn't getting as much sleep or sleeping as well and it started showing in my face. I stopped thinking about my goals and my forward movement in my new life. I got caught up again in this other person's problems, which all of a sudden now were my problems. I became anxious and worried about how this person was going to react to things, what was going to happen. I disconnected my lifeline to God.

I lost my focus. And to make matters worse I had already given my notice at work! Which was the right thing to do, but now doubt had slipped in. I was warring with myself over it. I was 100% sure I had completed what I was supposed to do at that job and it was time for me to leave and someone else to take over. Staying was not good for me or for the staff any more.

I hadn't told my husband yet, he had his own stress and problems to worry about regarding an important overseas trip he was scheduled to make on behalf of his family. But financial problems were making this difficult, another stress on me. I tried to rise above all of this. I tried to meditate and read. I made the promise each morning that I was not going to eat sugar or carbs, pasta or candy, whatever it was that was making by body feel 100 years old again. I tried the affirmations, but just couldn't get connected. I spent time alone on the back porch in the mornings trying to concentrate on the beautiful sky and clouds, the birds singing and the faint scent of gardenias. It didn't work.

My mind was cluttered and fragmented. I stopped thanking God for my perfect body and my perfection in His image. I didn't feel pretty or powerful or empowered or anything but – defeated. And I only had three days left on the job, the job that paid the rent and put food on the table and gas in the car.

How are you going to help others if you can't help yourself?

Wasn't this the reason why I was leaving my job in the first place? Because I knew, I mean I really knew what I was supposed to do next - mentor and coach others. Help them be empowered and reach their full potential. Give them encouragement and guidance, reassurance with a good kick in the pants when they needed it. Share everything I had learned and gone through over the last 58 years and make a difference in *their* lives. Teach self-reliance and motivation. And do this one-on-one, in the corporate world, in group settings, conferences and retreats. And even write and share all of it in a book or two.

What the hell was I thinking?

Maybe I had eaten too many green leafy vegetables and my blood sugar was low. If I was having a hard time sustaining this "thing" how was I going to help someone else sustain it? Was it not possible to live what you believed in this 2012 world? Are people still so stifled and full or fear?

For me, I had brought conflict back into my life, I let it happen. I didn't ask for it. But I didn't say, "No!" I let it come back, insidiously, like drops of water until the water is over your head and you are downing. Well, I can't swim and my head was definitely under water.

The battling voices in my head begin to grow louder, "What are you going to do about it!?" "What are you doing to do about it?!" I was letting these negative voices live in my head and heart rent free. They are free-loaders and I am giving them a free ride! I have to get them out! I have to evict them!

Then I got mad. I got mad at God. Boy isn't that stupid?

It wasn't his fault. He didn't do this to me. I had done it to myself. But since all the old behaviors were coming back I might as well let the "blame God" woe-is-me, back in too. As usual that wasn't working. So the next step down the spiral staircase was to entertain the even more dark and sinister thoughts of how things would be better if I wasn't around. I wouldn't have to think about things or deal with things, everything would just go away.

I was wallowing in my misery and came across something I had written months earlier when I was in my depths of depression:

"This isn't the world I grew up in." "This isn't my home anymore."

Funny, these were the words my mother said to me a few years before she died. I thought it was just the mutterings of an old person. Maybe it was true, but so what? Why and how would that make a difference to me? Then I realized this is not the world I grew up in either. This really doesn't feel like my home anymore. I now understand how my mother felt and why she lost interest in life - because I, too, am a stranger here and am finding it hard to hold on to my sanity and to my joy.

Both my parents are dead and I have no connection with the town or people where I grew up. All the people who watched me grow up and knew all those little things about me that no one else knew are gone. The story tellers and keepers of the traditions are gone. Now I am the story teller and the tradition keeper. But it is sad and hard. And who do I tell and what do I keep? These thoughts make me sigh and make me weary and very, very sad.

In my teens and 20's I thought I knew it all and had the energy to do it all. I was liberal and opinionated. By my 40's I realized I had been judgmental, revengeful and had missed out on a lot my life by just walking or running through it, not really participating in it. At 58 I realize that what I don't know, is by far, more vast than what I do know. And like the typewriter, I am becoming obsolete.

This is terrible!

I can't let this drag me down again. I refuse to drown in my own self pity. I will not be a victim of myself. And that's what it would be. There would be no one else to blame but me. And maybe this is where I had to get to. I *had* to get to the place where I take full responsibility for me. That I choose to live, *I choose life.* There is no one making me miserable or forcing me to be unhappy. I am doing it to myself.

This is the epiphany! It's about me! And I know from past experience that it is impossible to fail as long as I try!

So, I pulled out the tapes and CD's again and actually bought a new meditation set of CD's. And something on the second CD caught my attention. There's no right or wrong and no one can get this thing to work 100% of the time, it is a process. And just the awareness that I have "fallen off my wagon" is proof that I am living in the now and not just letting life happen to me. I realized I had a false sense of needing to "be perfect" and do things perfectly. And if I didn't I was failing, which is the exact opposite of the truth.

It's not about having to be perfect or do things perfectly, like there is a right or wrong way. The truth is we are perfect. We are perfectly made. We don't have to go around feeling less than, embarrassed or guilty, living up to some preconceived image or standard of "who or what" we should be. We can never live up to those standards. So we end up always feeling bad in some way about ourselves. Then we have to mask it with phony smiles and laughter or isolation so we don't have to deal with people.

Maybe we avoid mirrors so we don't have to see the person in the mirror. We can pretend we are someone else even if it's just for a little while. Or we eat, drink, do drugs, shop, purge or do something to alleviate the pain temporarily, but over time it destroys us.

Well, all of that sounds pretty profound. But, what does it really mean?

It means it is okay. For me, I am going to again stop dredging up the past (even if it was just 5 minutes ago). I am going to stop worrying about the future and what others think or of what might happen. Hell, I don't know what might happen in the next ten minutes. Anything could happen. And it could be good. AND that's the key. Or the key word, *good – or maybe GREAT!*

Right now, pay attention to right now, make right now the best "right now" possible!

Enjoy it! Savor it!

It will never come again. If you/I "we" eat a chocolate bar and it was not on our "healthy green-leafy vegetables" list for today, it's okay. Taste each bite and make it good. Make it great! Make it scrumptious! Because all we really have is now.

And do you know what happened when I realized all this?

Yup, you guessed it. I'm back.

Well, the "new" me is back. So what did I learn? I learned I could get through it. The world didn't come to an end. And I can feel good even with all my flaws, I can feel good. If I can, you can. We all can. When we feel good we can see the possibilities. Ideas flow. Excitement and enthusiasm fills the air, sparks fly!

We rise to align with our Source. For me, my Source is God, and since every minute of every day we are creating our life, we can make it good and meaningful and purposeful. That's the "Ah-ha" moment.

You and only you are creating your life. You and only you can create your future. And what you create is what you become. Who you let in or who you don't let in. Who you help or who you ignore. Opportunities you act on or ones you let pass you by. Are you being kind, loving, giving, forgiving, compassionate and honest to others, or maybe not? Either way, you are creating the world in which you live.

The principle of "We reap what we sow, what goes around comes around" or call it "The law of attraction" - it's just semantics. The truth is the truth no matter how politically correct you try to slice it.

If you want love, you have to give it. If you want respect, you have to respect yourself and others first. We always have to make the first move, and then the principle kicks in. We are the catalyst. We are the captain of our own fate. Again, its' the principle, it's the law.

Don't shoot the messenger!

Well, isn't this funny? Everything is exactly the same in my life as it was a day ago. But when my attitude and outlook changed, so did my life. I'm okay. And so is my life, no matter what. Like in my all-time favorite movie, "It's A Wonderful Life" when George realized he did have a wonderful life - so do I.

And remember, *"Every time a bell rings, an angel gets its' wings"*.

Wow, maybe I really am a philosopher. Maybe I need to change my name. All the really great philosophers have a one-word name - like Socrates, Aristotle or Confucius. Maybe I'll go by Sarah. That's what about a third of the people call me anyway. Somehow when they see Susan and Farah it gets stuck together and comes out Sarah. Honestly, this happens to me all the time.

So, I think I will start calling myself Sarah, too.

So Sarah, what have you learned?

I learned that I can be happy or sad no matter what is going on in my life. IT IS MY CHOICE! I can't blame anyone else. Good times will come. Bad times will come. That is just reality. *It is what I do with what comes, that makes the difference.*

I have always felt that it is impossible to fail. I mean we won't be successful all the time but that does not mean we have failed. As long as we try, there is no failure. Just steps of progression along the way, along that process to reach our goal. *No guilt...*

I've also realized that it has been important for me to get physically and healthy again. I am going to need it. Now, knowing that is a little intimidating.

What do you mean I am going to need it? Am I going to climb Mt. Everest? Or am I going to move mountains? I hope it's figuratively and not actually.

I look in the mirror and I do see a healthy, younger face. Hope I'm just not in denial about that younger part. But others have said it too. I believe that when we truly pursue change in all aspects of our life we *can* have it. It is important. Optimism conquers all. Oops, I think the saying is "love conquers all" but for today its optimism who is going to get the spotlight. Going back to Dr. Dyer and his lessons on intention, I decided to pull out my list of intentions I had written back in April. I read them and, Wow! I was really on fire.

My intention is to be kind and loving to myself, to others, all animals and the environment. "If you do it to the least of these – you do it unto me." - The Bible

My intention is to think and dwell on beautiful and perfect thoughts.

My intention is to be generous in thought and in resource to myself and to others, (I am just the vessel that things pass through, from God to others and back to God).

45

My intention is to ask, to believe and to receive ALL my blessings, (God owns everything and He loves me).

Well, who says I can't do this?

Nobody, that's who!

We truly can change past negative patterns, get unstuck from those old mindsets and learn new skill sets. Learn new ways of thinking so we can create a positive life for ourselves, not the negative one we have been living. Create a life in which we intentionally act and play an active role in. Not just spin our wheels reacting and let life happen to us, we can become victimless. Let's really hear that one.

We *can become victimless*! We <u>will</u> become victimless!

No one can make you a victim. Only <u>you</u> can label yourself a victim.

You have the power to be a victim or to not be one. It's that simple. Your life may not be what you want it to be *yet*. But you get to define who you are and you get to define what your life should look like. Start now. Don't procrastinate! Don't say you have to wash the car. Don't say you have to cook dinner or wash your hair. No excuses!

There are a lot of words out there to describe finding yourself. Finding your divine purpose or life purpose, finding your passion, becoming self-aware, the list goes on and on. What I know is that - we are what we believe. Our brains are funny like that. What ever we believe about ourselves, our life will back that up. I mean, we will say, do and act in such a way that it comes true whether it was true in the beginning or not. It will end up being true. This is *because our brains have to walk out what we believe.*

It's almost like we are separate from our brains. No, not multiple personalities, even though I myself talk to and answer

46

myself. Hey, how else am I going to get the right answer? Ha, ha, ha!

Our brains are like little computers. Whatever you program into it, is all it can give back to you. That's why our brains are so fascinating. It can block out trauma and put it way back in the deepest part of us. Or splinter off, and create another part of us, the one that deals with the pain. It can let us be so deeply affected by the trauma that we suffer pain, addictions and dysfunction in our life as a way to try to hide the pain. Or it may not bother us at all. Utterly amazing! And we never know which one it's gonna be.

Just like Forrest Gump's box of chocolates, "You never know what you're gonna get."

So the reality is we have to deal with what we have. Personally, I do like the Forrest Gump approach, a combination of optimism, trust, just do it and when it's done there's "*one less thing*" to worry about.

And a part of this truth is that, "*We do not see things as they are. We see them as we are.*" -The Talmud.

This means that it's our perception that gives us "our truth". If so, then we have to go one step further and quit just thinking about ourselves. We have to think about others because others' perception is "their truth". Think about that one for a minute. That's why people have such a hard time getting along. Why relationships are so tough and dealing with your family and co-workers is maddening sometimes. It's all about perception, everyone's perception. We have to be conscious of this and make an effort to work hard on relationships. Stay alert and find the real truth to any situation or controversy.

So, if we believe we are less than, or unsuccessful or unloved we must give up that belief. Give it up so that we can become all we can be. To become the person we were meant to be, that person who was created to live on this planet with a purpose. And it's about time that person got down to business, found out what that purpose is and started living it out!

And feel good. Just feel good. Start with that. Just feel good.

Tell yourself you feel good, act like you feel good and tell others you feel good. Your brain will believe it and it will become part of who you are. And you *will* feel good.

Again, we are what we believe.

It's like when you have hit too many curbs with your car and the tires are making your car pull to one side. You have to get your tires re-aligned. That's us. We need a re-alignment. Now, you can't go to the mechanic for that or to one of those drive-through fix-it places. You have to get on track with the possibilities and get rid of the obstacles. No limitations! The sky is the limit!

See it, believe it - achieve it!

Okay, Sarah. What have you been smoking?

Reframe. That's it!

Reframe, if you get stuck with lemons make lemonade. Don't pout and resist. Don't make drama. Don't use your emotions or angry thoughts to fuel the negative and distort the truth.

And what is the truth?

Well, it is that good things happen and bad things happen to everyone. What are you going to do when the good and the bad come? That's where the rubber meets the road. It's in that space that you are living your life. It's in that space you are creating your life. So in that space, are you creating the life you really want? Or are you letting the crap happen to you and then complaining about it, like you can't do anything about it? Aha!

Of course you can! Remember, you are what you believe!

So, what is our conclusion? What are we left with?

Well, if we take the Law of Attraction and the belief that we are like magnets and will get more of what we are thinking about; then it must be to our benefit to think about the positive and all the things *we do have*. This way we will get more, more of the good stuff! Rather than concentrating on and verbalizing our miseries, what we hate or what we don't have. Otherwise we will get more of that! And who the heck wants more of that?

REMEMBER...

That word keeps coming back to me. *Remember. Remember* why you are here. *Remember* your purpose. Maybe we have gotten it wrong. Maybe it isn't about searching for something that we haven't found yet. *Maybe it's remembering what we knew - but have now forgotten.*

Boy, is that deep or what? So, let's go with the assumption that this is true. Then, I must need to remember. Think. Think, reflect and remember.

What stirs up the passion in me? What stirs up the excitement in me, makes my body tingle and my mouth start to chatter away a mile a minute. What makes my eyes shine and brings an automatic smile to my face. What makes me hear the birds chirping, see the trees a little greener and the colors of the flowers more brilliant?

Discovering...

What do you mean? Discovering what?

Well, discovering something new.

Okay, but does that mean just bumping into new things that you haven't seen before?

No, not exactly. (See, I told you I hold these conversations with myself, this is what they look and sound like).

It's more like figuring it out.

Figuring what out, a mystery?

Yes, that's it!

It's like a mystery. Only not like a "who done it". It's more like a treasure hunt. And it's the richest and sweetest treasure that can be found. It's more like finding a way to make things better - a way to improve things, to reach higher heights and greater rewards, but only with people.

So...

CHAPTER SIX

"So When..."

I envy people who can remember things from when they were very young. They have these vivid memories from as far back as when they were babies. Not me. The first memory I have is around age three or four.

I see chickens. Yes, chickens.

My dad worked in the steel mill when I was very young, it was the 1950's. He was laid off quite a bit, so my parents took in my mother's uncle, Uncle Eli. I remember him and the chickens. The chickens chased me and tried to peck me and Uncle Eli smelled. I later found out it was the smell of old beer and wine. And until this day if I get a certain whiff of that combination it triggers the memory.

I guess the importance of remembering is that I used to be happy and recently I haven't been. I feel I have lost or have forgotten the real me and have been living my life in the shadow of that authentic me. That real "me" had a purpose. Let me readjust that - *has* a purpose.

And I've been intrigued by the realization that many people are saying the exact same thing but it doesn't sound the same because it's being said in different ways by different people at different times.

But, it's still the same thing: *Remembering our authenticity will get us back on the track of our train of life, before we derailed.*

So where do I begin for this soul search and finding those memories?

The first memory I have that surrounds this "authenticity thing" is one that happened when I was nine years old and in the 4th grade. I loved my 4th grade teacher. She was pretty, smart and self-confident. She was also tough, you couldn't get away with anything in her class.

This memory is going back quite a number of years when teachers could still paddle students as discipline. Well, she had a jar with tiny folded-up pieces of paper in it. And written on these tiny pieces of paper were the number of "whacks" of the paddle a student would get as punishment. I was a pretty good rule-follower back then, so I didn't have to put my hand in that jar too many times. But some students were less fortunate. One boy in particular - let's call him, Ron.

Ron was always doing something wrong; not doing his homework, not bringing his books to school and not reading the assignment so he could answer questions in class. As a result, Ron was always getting paddled.

Now the year went on and there was a stretch of time of "messing up" for Ron that defied logic. I mean it was unbelievable. He did so many things wrong in such a short period of time that his "whacks" added up to a really high number. Remember, I was nine at the time, so the actual number was somewhere in the mid twenties to mid thirties, but for a nine year old it seemed like a hundred.

Now the paddings weren't done every day. A special day was picked for this ritual every few weeks or so. Well, "whacking day" arrived and there were a number of students to get discipline and then, there was Ron.

There were always two teachers, the one "whacking" and the one "watching" the whacking, the witness or possibly the sense of reason, I don't know. But that day was a turning point. Ron was last and the wooden paddle with holes in it (I think that was so it would sting more) was being applied to his behind.

One, two, three... ten, eleven, twelve... nineteen, twenty... I started to feel sick.

I think a lot of us kids started to feel sick and really sorry for Ron. It was like the teacher was in a trance and couldn't stop, like she was a possessed person. I guess all of her frustrations with Ron had built up in her like a volcano and Mt. Saint Helen had just erupted!

The teacher-witness was looking uncomfortable and didn't know what to do. I can't remember at this point if she tried to stop my teacher or left the room to get someone else or what. All I know is that Ron got **all** of his whacks. He was crying and literally could not sit down. There was dead silence from everyone else and a thick layer of heaviness in the room. I can't explain that exactly. But you know the feeling, like there is an invisible substance in the room so dense you have to get a knife to cut through it. Well, that is what it was like.

Needless to say, there ended up being a lot of very negative outcomes for both the teacher and Ron. The fallout from that one day was felt for years to come.

Those few minutes had changed both of their lives, forever.

Lives would never be the same again. Mine, too.

I can remember it so vividly. I can hear the "whacks" and feel the sick feeling and see the horror in everyone's eyes even to this day. But most of all, I can remember the look of frustration, anger and raw fierceness in my teacher's eyes.

She couldn't stop! Even if she had wanted to, she couldn't. I mean she was intelligent and had always been firm - but fair. But something beyond her control had pushed her to the point of no return - and all her intelligence, knowledge and years of education had not prepared her in any way for that day.

Things were never the same in that class after that. I was too young to be able to analyze it, but my feelings changed for her. And even more than that, I began to think. Before that I never really thought about why Ron did these things. Maybe no one had. Kids were bad, disrespectful or lazy. Punish the bad behavior with the thought (and the hope) that the discipline would bring about good behavior.

Boy, that's pretty naïve. But you know, Ron didn't want to get whacked and for sure he didn't want to get whacked that many times. So there had to be reasons why he didn't do what he was supposed to do, right? I mean all he had to do was read, or bring his books to school and do his homework. Everyone else did, most of the time. What was the problem?

We found out later there were some tough things going on in his home at that time which probably had caused his behaviors. But why didn't someone find that out before the whacking? Even us kids, didn't know what was going on with him. And when Ron's defiant behavior kicked in and made matters worse, "Why didn't some of us kids try to talk with him?" I know we were only nine, *But isn't that old enough to make the effort to find out, to intervene?"*

It was like we were watching a TV program or movie and it just unfolded before our eyes, no interaction. Or maybe we were just happy it wasn't us. I don't know. But something was changed that day in me. I wanted to know the "why's". And so started my love affair with the "why's" and the "why-not's".

Now since I was an only child I had a lot of interactions with my parents and in many ways was treated as an adult. Discussions around the supper table included current events, interesting stories from past generations and the future decisions needing to be made. Quite often I had an equal part in this decision making. It was this unique combination that molded me into the person I was, or am. Hmmm...

I learned some really great things from my dad; love of sports, a super work ethic, an incredible giving spirit and a temper – let's say a short fuse. A short fuse at the end of a big firecracker – that was him!

From my mom I learned how to manipulate, my love of music, a secret desire to write and vain-"ness". Was she ever vain! Now to be honest, as a young woman she was pretty striking in her own way. She was very petite, only 4'11" and 100 pounds. I still have picture albums with hundreds of pictures others took of her, which of course she kept for posterity. I also learned from her how one tragic event in a person's life could alter that life forever.

My mom used to be a happy person. She had several sisters and brothers and most of them lived fairly close to us in a very small, close-knit town. It was so small that grades 2-12 were all in one building. Well, my mom and her youngest sister were really close. In fact, I really considered my aunt my second mom or maybe more like an older sister. The three of us did so many things together. She didn't have children, so I was her substitute.

She was a truly amazing person, but my aunt had some struggles. She was in an abusive marriage and back in the 1960's, which this was, divorce was not an option. Since my mom and my aunt were close, my mom knew things no one else did. I am sure my mom really didn't know what to do about all this and had no idea what was going to happen.

It was just a few weeks away from my 13th birthday and my aunt, her husband, my parents and I were planning a vacation together to Florida. I was so excited! She and my mother were talking on the phone one Saturday about it and all of a sudden my mom grabbed me and literally threw me in the car. She sped the car those few blocks to my aunt's house and pulled into the driveway with a screeching halt! She made me stay in the car as she went in the house. A short time later the ambulance showed up and my mom came out of the house crying and with a different face, one that I had never seen before - but the one I would get all too familiar with.

While talking on the phone my aunt had collapsed as a brain aneurysm burst in her head. I didn't' see her that day nor did I ever see her again. Back then they thought taking children to the hospital to visit sick relatives was too traumatic for them. But, in reality, with no real closure it took me thirty years and a counselor named Claire to finally say good-bye. Unfortunately, my mom never recovered. She turned slowly into a guilt-ridden, phobic, physically-sick woman, leaving her husband and daughter missing out on years of *"what could have been"*.

Since my dad was always jumping in his car and helping the neighbors in a crisis, or rummaging about the basement or garage looking for that nut, bolt or screw that someone needed - this rubbed off on me.

Another thing that rubbed off was his love of the "underdog". I don't care what person, team, animal or situation, he was always rooting for the underdog. I didn't understand it then but I now realize that was his way of encouraging others. Ironic, because by many people's standards he was an underdog himself; growing up without a mom, treated harshly by an abusive father and jealous stepmother. And if that wasn't enough he was practically blind in one eye due to a high school football injury.

But what a laugh he had! He loved life!

Wow, I guess I needed to remember all of that, hmmm...

So, my attraction to the "underdogs" and the "slightly odd personalities" had its humble beginnings as offspring of these two very different souls.

So, back to me...

Sometime around the 5th grade my own search and rescue began. Her name was, well - let's call her CC.

CHAPTER SEVEN

"So How...?"

CC.

Now CC and I were about ten or eleven. CC had bright orange hair, not red but orange, like a pumpkin. I had never seen orange hair before. It was naturally orange and didn't come from a box. And it was wild! Wildly all over her head, long and tangled. Her clothes were hand-me-downs and she talked very softly with a lisp.

She was not a very good reader and back then the teachers make you read, out loud. How come they always picked on the ones they knew couldn't read? I could never understand that. Did they really think that by making them stand up in front of the whole class, red as a beet and embarrassed was going to make them a better reader? Not logical. Wouldn't it have been better to coach someone one-on-one after class when no one was around until they got better? Then let them read and be successful to encourage self-confidence?

Oops, again I forgot. This was the 60's.

The kids made fun of CC. She sat at the end of the second row in the back and I was at the end of the first row across from her. She had the prettiest ocean-blue eyes. But most people didn't notice since she always was looking down, afraid to make eye contact.

Around that age girls start getting what I call "clicky" or "clickish". You know, establishing exclusive groups. The girls in our class followed suit and divided up into two groups. I can't remember the club names now, but I was supposed to be in one of them. No one wanted CC. she would be all by herself in the corner of the playground staring into space.

Well I thought that was pretty stupid, so C.C. and I had our own club. I don't remember much about it except I realized at the age of eleven that clubs with all girls in it were a real pain and I didn't want to belong to one. I don't know if I made a difference in C.C.s' life or not. But since this stands out so vividly in *my* mind, it made a difference for me. Maybe it is one of those occurrences in life that helps us remember our purpose has been with us from the beginning.

So, life went on. By the time I got to high school it was the late 60's and for you history buffs; mini skirts, The Beatles and bucking "The Establishment" was definitely the "in" thing to do. I began to get more opinionated and vocal when I saw something I didn't like. It seemed like there was always something to stand up and speak out for.

All of a sudden I started to notice boys and well, for the next several years all my attention went into trying to get them to notice me. Graduating high school, getting a job and getting married filled up the next few years. And over the next ten years I was a wife and then a mother *and forgot to be a person*. But somewhere underneath a big pile of clothes in a locked closet in the basement, there lurked this very large boiling pot of stifled hormones. A caldron bubbling over with thoughts and dreams...

I had two escapes. One was to dream and fantasize. Boy I made a career out of that one! I would literally make up soap operas in my head featuring me at the star. Usually I would pick a famous person or movie star who would fall in love with me and sweep me off my feet. Poor Ted Kennedy (he was young and good looking then), was my obsessive focus for years. The plots would be very detailed and I would steal away any time I could to day dream or night dream my life away. This "other world" became so real to me, and I needed it so desperately, that my real life seemed like *the dream.*

I began to just walk through my reality as quickly as I could so I could spend more and more time in my fantasies. I now realize that is why there are whole blocks of time I can't recall, I was only there physically. I wasn't there mentally living my life. I was just "roboting" through it.

My other escape was the cemetery. I know that sounds morbid but it really isn't. Our town had an awesome cemetery. Beautiful trees and flowering bushes, wild flowers and unique stone markers were everywhere. There's an older section and a newer section, I particularly liked the older section. It felt like I was on a treasure hunt. It wasn't exactly treasure, but it felt like it and I needed it!

Many of the graves and tombstones were from the 1800's. Some of them had pictures of the deceased in ornate silver frames attached to the stones. I wandered through and befriended children, parents and grandparents - their pictures stately and solemn. This was my quiet time, it was important. It was like something was pulling me there and I would walk and listen to the quietness, watch and wait.

Watching and waiting for what, you ask?

Now this is where things really begin to get interesting...

Ever since I could remember I believed there was something greater than me. I believed there was a God but that's about it. I went to church on the holidays and tried to be a decent person but I had never done any real soul searching or had any great spiritual awakenings. Nothing out of the ordinary ever seemed to happen to me. But it was funny, the only real place I felt peace or closeness to God was out in nature or in that dang cemetery.

So, I began to talk to him there.

Mostly I told him I knew he existed but I didn't believe in all that bible stuff; Jonah inside a whale, Noah and the ark and well, Jesus. I mean that rising from the dead thing was too much for me. I didn't want to insult God and I told him that, but really whoever wrote that stuff, "Why did they have to make it so far-fetched?" If God really wanted us to believe it, he could have made it more believable, right?

We held a lot of one-sided conversations in that cemetery.

I can remember the day so clearly, the last day I lectured God and gave him my opinion on how he should have done it. My husband and daughter had gone to church and I went to the cemetery, that was my church. And I talked and talked and God listened. I can just imagine how it had to look and sound to God. He was either laughing so hard he was crying over *me* telling *him* what he should do and should have done or else he was holding both sides of his head because he had another migraine from listening to me, for the umpteen time, complaining. Either way it had to be a silly sight.

I think that day God just got tired of me and said, *"Okay, I'll show you."*

And he did.

My daughter was about seven years old and one night we were at a PTA meeting and we ran into one of our neighbors. I knew she had just finished going to school for something and had gotten a job at one of the local hospitals. So I flagged her down and asked her about it. She started to describe what she did and it sounded good, plus it paid good money. Now I think she thought I already knew what she did, so she started *halfway* through the description of the job, (I missed the most important part - the beginning). At least that is how I justified what happened next.

So, the next day I called the technical college where she had gotten her training. Now, this part honestly did happen but you probably are going to think I am making it up because I am writing this book and need a really good story. But honestly, it happened just like this - I didn't hear everything they said to me on the phone.

I know we all have selective hearing, but this went far beyond that. I specifically didn't hear the one word that would have made all the difference. It would have stopped me from the thing that shaped the next 25 years of my life. That one word was "nurse".

You see growing up I didn't know what I wanted to do with my life but there was one thing I did know, I didn't want to be a nurse. If fact, on the playground at school when we would go around the circle and everyone would say what they wanted to be when they grew up, I would say, "Anything but a nurse!"

I didn't know everything a nurse did but I knew it had something to do with sick people and hospitals and those were two things I was not going to have anything to do with. So I guess I shouldn't be surprised that I had blocked the word "nurse" from my vocabulary. Whenever "nurse" was spoken or in writing in front of me, there was a blank - a space of nothingness. Sounds crazy I know, but this is where God began to intervene in my life.

Back to the phone call. I called, requested the information, got the information in the mail, signed up for the free test

Susan Chuey Williams Farah

exam, passed the exam, got my parents to pay the $1,800.00 up-front, non-refundable fee and then showed up on the first day of class. I did all of this without realizing I was going to be a nurse.

Ludicrous you say?

Impossible?

You can say whatever you want but it's true. I went into the building, stood in line with the rest of the students and got a boxful of books. I then proceeded into the auditorium, sat down and waited. The director of the program got up and started to talk about how this was the first day of a rewarding path and career, blah, blah, blah...you know all the stuff they gotta tell you the first day.

When she got done I dragged this box of heavy books up to the second floor (no elevators) and sat down in a classroom filled with about 40 other women and one man. Several instructors introduced themselves and then one of them started to talk about what we would be learning. Through this ocean of blurred words I heard the word, "shot" or maybe it was injection. *That, got my attention!*

My antennas went up!

I was now like a blood-hound hot on the trail. With my very keen sense of hearing, (ha, ha, ha), I zoomed in like Sherlock Holmes, nothing was going to get past me now. And to my horror I heard a detailed description of the duties of a nurse. Or more precisely, the things I would be learning to do as a nurse and then, actually be expected to do: *"AS A NURSE!"*

I had a panic attack right there in row number five, the next to the last seat. My heart was beating out of my chest, my eyes were like saucers, my palms were sweating, I couldn't breathe and I was ready to throw up.

63

Somehow I made it to the end of the day. I don't remember anything else that happened. I got in the car and starting crying. I cried all the way home and was still crying when I walked through the door. Hysterically I told my husband everything that had happened and how I wasn't going back. I couldn't do it, I didn't want to do it and how the hell did this happen? How could I have signed up and paid money to become a nurse when the last thing on earth I wanted to be - was a nurse!

Sounds like a scene from a soap opera, doesn't it? If this was a movie I would have paid good money to go and see it. What was I going to do? I then read the fine print on the enrollment form. No refunds. No go to class, no pass course - no refund"ey" the m.o.n.e.y.!

Again the crying...

Now $1,800.00 in the early 80's was a lot of money and it was my parent's money. So being the responsible people we were, my husband and I decided, "Oh well, at least go the next day and see what happens." Pretty sophisticated, right?

So I went the next day and the day after and the day after that. The class part, the studying and the tests were pretty easy for me. My brain was still intact and I had always been a good test taker. I also met three women that would turn into life-long friends. That was great, but looming in the back of my mind was the knowledge that very soon the time to actually touch and care for patients was approaching. It was coming; circling like a buzzard waiting for it's next meal. Circling, and getting closer and closer.

Now our instructors were really wise. They had worked with "want-to-be" nurses for a long time and they could read us like a book. There were four of them and all very different. Two were awesome, one was okay and one was MEAN! I hoped every day that I wouldn't get stuck with the mean one when it was time to go to the hospital and do clinical. This was in the 80's when people still went into the hospital to get tests done and to die.

At first we just made beds, took blood pressures and things like that. I was a nervous wreck! Hard to think that someone could get petrified about making a bed, but you had to do it perfectly or you would fail that task. Soon the dreaded day was upon me. I was going to have to actually touch a patient, take care of a patient – *take care of a sick person!* I wanted to run and hide.

I had been assigned to one of the cool instructors, thank goodness. It was the only good thing. My patient was a little old man who was basically comatose and was there to die, probably in the next few days. Well, at least if I messed up he couldn't tell anyone. That thought kept running through my brain over the next two days.

At this point, all we were trained to do was give a bath, give a back rub (this is when everyone got a back rub), change the bed and do vital signs (blood pressure, pulse, temperature and respirations). I was terrified! It felt like I was going to faint.

Well, at least I was in the right place for that!

It took me forever to give that care. It took me about an hour just to get the nerve to touch him. But an amazing thing happened. By the end of the second day as the instructor popped her head in the door of the patient's room, I was singing, comforting him and gently rubbing his frail little body with lotion. I was calm and happy. As the instructor's and my eyes locked this little "I'm so smart" smile appeared on her face, she nodded her head and left the room. And that is how the girl who; didn't like sick people, didn't like hospitals, afraid of old people and wanted to be "anything but a nurse" - became a nurse and loved it.

Now you can say many things to try to explain why I blocked out the "nurse" word in this whole experience. But I know why. This was the only way God could get me where he needed me to be.

Chalk one up for God!

It also gave me the opportunity to find my passion for encouragement, advocacy and, quite frankly, the love of taking charge, being in charge and leading. So, I and my three student friends, now also graduated, resurrected the Choffin School of Practical Nursing Alumni Association. Sounds pretty impressive, doesn't it? I, of course, jumped in as President and my three cohorts fell in as vice president, secretary and treasurer. We had meetings, supported each other and on occasion had the opportunity to encourage students who were on that rocky road to becoming a nurse.

I had the honor to be the speaker at one of the commencement ceremonies and learned that being open and honest and sharing the real part of yourself is what motivating and inspiring people is all about. Using your words to help them believe they can do it. They can do it, too. They can do it better.

I used the example of what I always had used for myself. I called it, "The Mirror".

The "Mirror" is seeing your self actually doing it, saying it or having it. Envisioning yourself walking down the aisle with the diploma in your hand or getting the passing grade in the mail, seeing it happen. Maybe I got this from all those Walt Disney movies. You know when the old hag would bring out the mirror and talk to it, "Mirror, mirror on the wall who's the fairest of them all?" But with a twist, use it for good not for bad, "Two for good, one for bad."

Oops, there I go again, loved that Dustin Hoffman in "Rainman". Tom Cruise was no slouch either.

Well a few years went by and I realized I needed to go to college and get my RN. So I worked and did that while playing at being wife and mother. I encouraged my three nursing school buddies to do the same. I was a registered nurse so logically I should go where the big money is, right?

So I went to work at one of the local hospitals on the 3-11 pm shift. I had just left behind my wonderful, beautiful, elderly souls and everyday had to leave my house at 2:30 pm and spend the evening away from home. I had left everything that was important to me and every night I cried. I cried going to work, I cried at work and I cried on the way home from work - every day.

This was a lesson hard learned.

Just because something is logical, looks good on paper or is what everyone else thinks you should do, doesn't mean it is the right thing for *you* to do. This one decision put a whole chain of events in place that would hurt a lot of people and mess my head up for a long time. Let's call this my "screwed up" period. You know, Van Gogh had his "blue period" well Susan had her "screwed up" period. And it was also blue with depression, red with anger and almost every other color in the rainbow!

While I was crying on the 3-11 pm shift my husband was having an affair with his high-school sweetheart. Talk about low blow to the old self-esteem, mine went into the dirt. It was flushed down the toilet. I'm not going to talk much about this or give all the dirty details except to say initially I hid my hurt well. I found out, I confronted, stood back, played the counselor and listened to him talk about her. I guess I thought, "Oh crap" I don't know what I thought. *It was just stupid!*

But I did it. I listened when he said he loved me but he was confused, he was this, he was that, blah, blah, blah. And

I listened all the way up to the point when he told me they went shopping and she used a crystal to choose between two blouses she was looking to buy. The crystal told her which one to buy.

That did it!

This guy that I had been married to for twelve years wanted to be with a woman who toted around a crystal to make decisions for her? No way. I mean, really... "No way!"

I was not going to let my daughter be exposed to that! And besides, no one was going to dump me, If there was going to be any dumping, I was the one who was going to do it! I was going to be the dumper not the "dumpee"!

And this is where I lost my mind. I lost my sanity. I lost control.

Again, I made decisions that would negatively impact many lives for many years. I used guilt and manipulation to get him to stay with me. I pretended things were wonderful, sought revenge with an affair of my own and then pulled a surprise divorce on him when he least expected it. He was clueless.

Life was never the same for any of us.

Later, I had to do a lot of amends. But I also realized somewhere along the line that things happen for a reason. And without all of that happening I wouldn't be the person I am today and I don't think I would have had the opportunities I have had. I know one thing for sure, all of that stopped me from living in my head. **I didn't have time!** And frankly, real life suddenly had become more like a soap opera than the stuff I had been making up in my head. Go figure!

So where are we?

Oh yeah...

The next thing that happened is the reason why I am sitting at the computer writing this to you today. My pent-up emotions, hormones and soul searching were about to have a head-on collision with an immovable force, let's call him, T.

My immoveable force: Tom #2.

CHAPTER EIGHT

"So Where Did I...?"

I fell in love. I fell down a well. Maybe I should have fallen down a well and not in love. It would have been a lot less painful and a shorter way up from the bottom. I was divorced and stuck with years of pent up hormones and yearning. So. I did what any 36 year-old woman would do? I went wild.

I have to look back at this period with mixed emotions. There are many things I wished I hadn't done. Then there's the part of me that understands and says, "Give her a break!" And I do.

Why I compare falling in love to falling down a well is that I fell in love with a person addicted to drugs. A funny thing, I used to have prejudices, quite a number of them. I have less now because a force wiser than me compelled me one by one to face these prejudices head on. After the first few the light bulb went off, so I try really hard not to have prejudices anymore.

Life has a tendency to do that to you, and I know there is a lot of laughing going on up there. The other thing I realized in dealing with my prejudices is that somehow when I got to the other side of it, people would show up in my life with that same situation. They would just show up on my door step or

I would bump into them at the mall, in the restroom - *or I would hire one of them.* I would be faced with an opportunity to share or encourage them in some way.

That's the "ironical" business, God's sense of humor...

I used to have three major prejudices: people with addictions – "Hey, just stop", women in abusive situations "Hey, just get out", and people with depression "Hey, just get out of bed."

Ha, ha, ha! I got all three.

But first, the love...

I really fell head over heels. I was naïve, I grew up in a small town and thought everyone was like me. So, here's "me" - when I tell you something you can believe it and when I tell you I will do something, I will. Funny to find out at this stage in the game not everyone is the same as me. Basically, I was an enabler before I found out what an enabler was.

I believed. I gave time, energy and money. I made excuses and I totally turned my life upside down. Because there was one thing he had that I wanted - it was his *passion,* and *faith.* It mesmerized me. It drew me in. I wanted to believe in something beyond a shadow of a doubt like he did. I had too! And God in his humor used the obsession of a man to bring me to the door and then patiently waited for me to knock. Besides, he looked like a young Al Pacino. And I'm a sucker when it comes to Italian men – especially someone looking like a *young* Al Pacino.

And knock I did. It was September 1993 when I let God in. And as my personality always does, I did it 150%. I went from believing almost nothing to believing everything in unlimited quantities and possibilities; Noah and the Ark, Jonah and the Whale and the parting of the Red Sea. Most importantly I believed Jesus as my Savior and not just a great teacher. I believed everything like a child, which was fortunate *and* highly useful for what was coming next!

Loving someone with addictions will make you do one of two things: hate the person and the addictions or learn to love the person and hate the addictions. Either way, you have to stop blaming them for all the bad things that have now slapped you in the face and landed in your life. *You* have to take the responsibility for allowing it to happen and saying "yes". Which is why all that stuff is really in your life anyway, you know. Once you get to that point of responsibility, (if you ever do) you have a choice to make. Cut bait and run, or stay.

I did both, but I am getting ahead of myself.

Let's talk about some miracles. I really needed some miracles at this point in my life. I was divorced, dating a wonderfully addicted guy, fighting with my parents over this wonderfully addicted guy and doing a poor job raising my daughter. It gets worse. I was still enmeshed in that old affair trying to get out but the man wouldn't let me - and now it was turning abusive.

I was also reeling from the feelings of guilt from a past abortion, then add to that a sprinkling of "sowing some wild oats" - going to bars and flirting. Hey, I needed reassurance I was sexy. And, oh yes, using bulimia, starving myself and excessive exercising to get thin. Sounds a little out of control, doesn't it? I made some of those movie stars look like Snow White!

You know you have lost your mind when after taking Syrup of Ipecac, throwing up and dry heaving for hours (but losing five pounds), you do it again. Luckily the second time was much worse and that little bell finally rang inside my head and started blaring "This is just **too crazy**!" I didn't do that one again.

No, I just switched to laxatives and diuretics. I used to look in the mirror and think, "If I lose enough weight and get sick someone will have to realize something is wrong and help me."

Isn't that crazy?

I couldn't ask for help. But really, who could I ask?

The depression got deeper and deeper. My relationship with my daughter was getting worse and as the progression of addiction goes, my wonderfully addicted boy friend was now is prison. I couldn't think. I couldn't remember things and half of what I could remember didn't make any sense. Looking back I can see how this was my parents worse nightmare. Add a pinch of "on-fire with God" to the recipe and Today's Special on the menu I served up was, "disaster"!

Okay... now the miracles.

It was Saturday and my daughter and I were doing our own thing around the apartment. We had moved from a lovely three bedroom house to a one bedroom and a couch, second-story apartment on a busy street in a neighboring town. My daughter decided to go to the mall and said to me, "Remember, mom, if you let Teddi (the dog) out, please put her on the leash." I had a bad habit of not doing this and she knew it. And off she went.

About an hour later the dog had to go out. So, because I am just so darn mature I take her out without her leash thinking, "I will just stand right by her and when she is done doing her business I'll bring her in." Great plan, huh.

So, while I was doing all of this the phone rings. I instinctively run up the stairs to answer the phone. I talked a few minutes and then came down the stairs to find; NO DOG!

The dog is gone. The dog is no where in the yard. I start running around yelling her name and then I hear the thunder, the very loud thunder. Did I tell you the dog is terrified of thunder and runs and hides? No, I forgot to tell you just like I forgot to put the dog on the leash!

Just about this time my daughter pulls into the driveway with her boyfriend and I have to tell her what I've done. She becomes hysterical... I don't blame her. She loves this dog. This dog has been with her for eight years, through all the crap her father and I have put her through. This is her best friend and now her best friend is lost, scared, wet (it is now raining), and it's getting dark.

My daughter and her boyfriend get in the car and go house to house and street to street for hours trying to find Teddi. They describe her; a brown poodle, weighing about eight pounds and has ribbons with red and white poke-a-dots on her ears. They gave everyone our address and phone number.

Hours later my daughter came home, she would not even look at me. She was disgusted. I know the thought running through her head was, "How irresponsible!" And she was right. At 17 my daughter was more responsible than her 41 year-old mother. She didn't speak to me. The next day she didn't speak to me. Again, her and her boyfriend went out to look for the dog. By this time it had stopped raining, but still no sign of Teddi.

I was beside myself. Even I, who had spent the last several years being self-absorbed, selfish and immature, now realized what a complete louse I was. I was pacing and talking to myself. Then somewhere in the midst of the talking I started crying out to God. I admitted to him that I had been wrong and because of my actions the relationship with my daughter was being destroyed.

I then told God that I knew he was a miracle worker and he could do anything. I believed that then, and I believe that now. I also told him I knew that there were so many more important things in the world: war, hunger, starving children, epidemics and natural disasters - but honestly to me and my daughter, this was the most important thing in our lives. And if he could just bring the dog back, I promised I would know it was a miracle and I would not be afraid to tell everyone and anyone who would listen.

Then I did a crazy thing, I told God I was going to sit down on the porch step and not move until he brought the dog back. Like, I said before, like a child – child-like.

About 30 seconds go by and a van pulls up in the driveway. I didn't recognize the van but I saw a man driving, a woman sitting next to him and yes - a brown poodle with ribbons and those silly red and white poke-a-dots on its ears. Teddi!

Thirty seconds + Teddi = miracle!

This is my dog miracle story and I will tell everyone and anyone exactly as I told God I would do.

Here's the rest of the story which is just as amazing.

The man and woman who pulled up in my driveway were husband and wife. Every Saturday they drove 25 miles to visit her mom (she lives on the next street). So, on Saturday they were there when my daughter and her boyfriend knocked on the door and told them about her lost dog.

After their visit they go home as usual. The next morning the wife wakes up and says, "Let's go visit mom again today." This turns into a discussion because they never go two days in a row. But after about an hour of trying to come up with an excuse not to go, they decide to make the trip.

As they were driving down the street to her house the husband sees this brown poodle trotting down the street and says to his wife, "That's the dog the little girl was talking about yesterday, let's stop and pick it up." The wife is unsure and doesn't want to grab the dog thinking what if it is the wrong dog. But the husband insists, "It has to be the one, it has the ribbons in its ears." So they stop, he grabs the dog and because they both remember the address (ha, ha, ha) pull into my driveway thirty seconds after I sat down on the steps and told God I wasn't moving until he brought that darn dog back. So in pulls the van with Teddi, her head hanging out the window, smiling at me and saying, "What's up?" (I made that last thing up).

I was speechless.

I barely was able to utter "thank you" as the man handed Teddi to me. I think I tried to give him a reward for finding her but he said no. After they left I looked up and told God, "Okay, you got me." And I kept my promise. To this day almost 20 years later, I tell this story to all the people that God puts in my path.

My daughter came home and gradually things began to get better between us. I would love to say that from that point my life was smooth sailing but stuff like that only happens in movies. I was still me and my life was still in chaos, but now God was in charge and all those compromises I used to make he was now squeezing out of my life.

I still kept looking in the mirror and hoping someone would see I was slowly killing myself. I had a panic attack. It was so bad I had to lock myself in my office at work and sit on my hands for an hour, so I wouldn't run out the door, jump in my car and drive to New York City.

Why New York City? I don't know, that is what the panic was telling me to do.

I finally went to see my doctor. He took one look at me and said, "Oh, my God, what happened to you?" I think he thought I had cancer. I just told him a few symptoms and a little bit of what was happening in my life. He gave me a standard test measuring depression and I flunked it. I scored somewhere between a high moderate and a severe.

He looked me straight in the eye and said, "I should put you in the hospital right now, but instead I am going to give you some medicine. If this doesn't help you within seven days I am admitting you to the hospital!"

I think it was the word "hospital" that clicked. You would think that since for months I had been destroying my body and wanting someone to realize it, that this would have been good news. But somewhere down deep that old message kicked in, *"Warning! Warning! Danger! Danger! Go hospital - BAD!"*

I got scared. I really didn't want to go to the hospital. I didn't want to be sick. So I got the prescription filled. This too, I am going to classify as a miracle. It was the only way God could get my attention. The miracle drug for me was Prozac. It was amazing!

A funny side-note before we continue.

My girlfriend was divorced and having a lot of problems too, and had been put on Prozac the same week I was. So we compared notes. We had a standing joke going for years, "BP & AP" – before Prozac and after Prozac.

Example: *You don't have money to pay your bills. BP (before Prozac,) you are frantic - picturing being thrown in the street and living in the gutter, AP (after Prozac), "Who cares?" "Let's go shopping and get an ice cream cone!"*

And you remembered where you stashed $200.00 for a rainy day.

I gained back all the weight I had lost and an additional twenty, but I could think again. I had to do a lot of apologizing. Do you know how you know when you have been sounding stupid at work? You find important reports you sent to your boss with words scratched out and things that looks like bunches of scribbles written all over them. Again, much apologizing.

I broke up with the man I previously had an affair with and lost my job. Don't ask me to explain that connection. So I was out of a job but in a good way. Again, I considered this a miracle too, it was just not how I wanted it to happen. But I had been praying for God to get me out of that situation. So when you pray, remember to be specific, otherwise God will do it how *he* wants to.

This next story is a BIG miracle and since it is connected to that giving and encouraging part of me, it's the catalyst that catapults me back in the flow of the person I used to be. The person I need to be again.

The sister-in-law of my BP/AP friend is a very unique person. She finds herself in very i-n-t-e-r-e-s-t-i-n-g situations. So, when I met her and began to spend time with her, presto! My life became more interesting. Let's call my extraordinary friend, "K".

Now K. is an advocate for everything and everyone. And when God did the class on "boundaries" she was in the bathroom. Needless to say, K. always had about ten projects going on at the same time, I don't know how she kept them straight. I couldn't. But sometimes, something stupendous would happen, like our trip to Mexico.

K. had made a trip to this little village in Mexico, I can't remember how she found herself there originally, but she stumbled across this village. The people were very poor and needed help and she decided, *she* was the one to help them. That *she* was the only one who could. The help that was needed most was healthcare and the supplies to provide that care.

Surprise! I was running a DME (durable medical equipment) company at the time (what a coincidence), and had supplies. But more importantly, had contact with a lot of suppliers. So we hatched the trip to Mexico. I spent several months contacting doctors, hospitals, other DME's and wholesalers for samples, medical supplies and equipment and K.'s job was everything else; get the place to store the supplies, people to help box it, get us and all this stuff over to Mexico and then get the stuff in the hands of the volunteer doctor and the people who needed it.

Seems simple, right?

Well, the first part went great. She got a big building, boxes, able-bodied helpers and I got the "stuff". We ended up with 40 boxes, all shapes and sizes filled with medical supplies and equipment. It was a lot!

K. booked the trip and told me she was working with the Red Cross to get everything over there. The trip was all planned and I didn't ask any more details, I was just along for the ride.

So, K. gets a very large truck, we load the boxes, get our luggage and proceed to the airport. She had arranged everything so I didn't even know what airline I was about to fly to Mexico on.

Side-bar: don't bury your head in the sand, ASK!

We are now at the ticket counter, this is back in the 90's when you still went to the airport and stood in line to get things done. The very big truck with all the boxes is outside illegally parked in the no-parking zone. It is at this precise moment that K. explains to the lady behind the ticket counter, *"Oh, by the way, we have these 40 boxes of supplies that we have to bring to Mexico with us so we can set up this clinic because the recent hurricane wiped out their village and they need help desperately and the supplies that have been going in have been confiscated and black-marketed so we need to take them in personally."*

She said this really fast all in one breath with NO commas! I think she thought if she said it really fast the lady would be confused and just say okay. Or maybe she would get amnesia and let us go through with the 40 boxes. I don't know what she thought or if she had a plan, but she did have a letter on Red Cross stationary saying that we were going to this little village in Mexico with supplies for the people there to help set up a clinic.

Oh, wait. I forgot to tell you the best thing. Besides all of this, we had no money to pay extra for these boxes.

Now K. was a spiritual person. Her beliefs and mine were slightly different but I had no doubt that she truly believed she was on a mission. The lady behind the counter looked dumbfounded and then proceeded to say, "No" - again, and again, and again!

It was now very close to boarding time. K. calmly turns to me and says, "Go ahead and get on the plane."

What?!

She wanted me to get on the plane? Was she out of her mind? She looked at me very sternly and again repeated, "Go get on the plane." So, I went and got on the plane.

I am now sitting in a seat on the plane by myself. I have no idea where I am going, except I do know the name of the village. I know no one there, I have no contacts there or numbers to call. And I have no money because K. is holding everything or at this point I guess she is holding everything. I don't even know.

The stewardess starts to talk and demonstrate the life jackets, etc... No K.

The pilot gets on the overhead and starts talking about the flight. No K.

I am beginning to have an anxiety attack. My palms are sweating, my face is red, my ears are ringing and all kinds of crazy thoughts are going through my head. I decide to look out the window to see if I can distract myself and all I see is the conveyor belt loading the last piece of luggage onto the plane.

The "buckle your seatbelts" sign comes on. Panic!

"I have to get off this plane!"

Then out of the corner of my eye I see the conveyor belt start moving again and one of our 40 boxes is being loaded on the plane. Then the second, then the third... until all 40 boxes were loaded. I just sat there with my mouth gaping and watched it happen.

I didn't even notice K, sit down next to me until I heard her voice say, *"No problem."*

I turned to her and she just smiled, closed her eyes and took a nap.

How could she sleep! I could barely breathe! Little did I know she was just resting up for the next round!

We landed in Mexico at this very small airport. K. whispers to me, "I don't know what's going to happen."

"What do you mean you don't know what is going to happen?" I said.

She just walked straight ahead, so I followed her. We found ourselves inside the airport amongst a lot of men in uniform. All 40 of our boxes were there, pushed toward the back of the room. K. told me that this was where the major problem had been for supplies coming into the country. They never got to the people who needed the help, they got this far and were confiscated and sold on the black market. But she had a plan and *ours* was going to be different.

The plan?

She had a friend whose sister-in-law lived in one of the neighboring towns and she was going to meet us there and talk with the men in uniform. Oh, and by the way, we didn't know the language either - so *we* were of *no help*.

That's it? That was the plan?

How was one lady going to convince all these men to let us through with all these boxes of medical supplies and equipment which could be sold for thousands of dollars?

Did she really think was going to work?

Great! Besides that, she wasn't there.

The men moved towards the boxes and K. took out her letter from the Red Cross, waved her arms and repeated over and over "Red Cross" "Red Cross". They were not impressed. They started to open the boxes. We were goners. They tore open the first three boxes, bandages fell out. Luckily they had started with the minor items, but just a few boxes away were the medications and equipment - the serious ticket items.

Then I heard a commotion on the other side of the room. There was this little Mexican lady about 5 foot tall waving her arms and speaking very loud and very fast. She began to argue with several of the men. She pointed to a small adjacent room where a fellow sat with a big hat behind a big desk. I assumed he was the chief or captain or some high-ranking official, he had the hat. They escorted her in and then the *really* loud arguing went on. By now they were ready to open the fifth box and this one, well, when they opened this one, it would be all over.

Just then the captain or chief flew out of his office, barked something to the men and went back into his office. The men stopped, pointed to the door and said, "Go." I think that was in a universal language.

The little Mexican lady ran over to us and said, "Hurry". And we did! We didn't stop to think or to worry that any minute the man with the big hat would change his mind. A flatbed was waiting outside and we loaded the boxes on that truck lickity-split and got the heck out of there!

Miracle #2...

Now I am sitting with the boxes on the back of the flat-bed and thinking, "Okay, I get it. I don't understand it, but I get it." And I did. There was a force greater than me or any of the people involved in charge and I wanted him on my side. Or rather, I wanted to be on his side.

Over the next few days we helped the volunteer doctor set up a clinic in a small one-room building the size of a small bedroom. It was crammed full of supplies and she was *thrilled!* By the end of that first day she was already seeing patients, handing out medicine and patching-up cuts and scraps.

Later that night we ended up at her hut located right on the gulf, eating hummus and sharing stories. After dinner we walked along the water, it was peaceful and we felt good about all we had been able to accomplish.

Now we still had a few days left before we were scheduled to go back home and as usual K. had the next day all planned. We would meet up with someone she had met on one of her previous trips (surprise), who of course, was also a unique individual.

The plan was to take the next two days, rent a little car, travel into the jungle, stay overnight in a motel that used to be a monastery, then the next morning go snorkeling. Now, I don't put my head under water unless I am taking a shower, so I wasn't quite sure how this all was going to work out for me. But again, I was along for the ride.

We rented the car and rode for miles further and further into the jungle. We saw first hand how many people had been living since the hurricane. No electricity. No running water. Just huts made from sheets of tin, propped up with poles and with just a fire to keep them warm, cook their food and give them light at night. All of a sudden I began to get really thankful for my life back in the good old United States.

We got lost, but right before dark we found the place, it almost looked abandoned. There was an inn-keeper of sorts, but we were the only paying customers. We brought our luggage to our rooms, met together for a small meal then gathered in our room, (K.'s and mine) to unwind before going to bed. We were talking when all of a sudden I noticed that my leg felt funny. I looked down and a bolt of fear shot through me!

There it was. On the bottom portion of my leg - a two-inch long scrape with a red streak four inches long. I had scraped my leg on something along the water earlier that day and didn't know it. Now infection had already set in and I realized not only was I very tired but felt a little warm too. It was clear I was beginning to run a fever.

Now, we are out in the jungle, no one else in this motel, there is no doctor, no hospital and it is midnight. This is when I really needed a miracle - for me!

Well, we were in a monastery, weren't we? Should be a great place for a miracle, right?

So, the four of us prayed. Believe me, each prayer was really different - but the point was the same. And I did take some Tylenol, I did have that. Just to think, all that medication back at the clinic and none with us. How ironic!

So, we did the only thing we could do - we went to bed. And yes, in the morning the red streak was gone, the redness was gone, the swelling was gone and the scratch was almost invisible.

I didn't question it. I didn't even let an inkling of curiosity hit my brain. I just smiled and said, *"No problem"*. I had learned what I was supposed to learn on that trip. Three miracles in less than a week!

I was to have several other amazing adventures with K. over the next few years. She continued to take trips to Mexico and then added Native Americans in the Dakotas and an orphanage in Central America to her list of projects.

She got the Army to add her "packages of love" to their flights when they were flying near her project areas. She was able to get volunteers, doctors, nurses, dentists and everyday people to go on these trips with her and donate their time and talents. She put together a non-profit with newsletters, outreaches and amazing testimonials. She was and still is an awesome and interesting individual, she never takes "no" for an answer. To her there is always a way, I agree. K. was someone God put in my life to teach me. She did more for me than I ever did for her and her projects. I am sure that is how everyone who knows her thinks of her and I hope I can achieve even a little of what she has achieved.

This is the last story I will share with you and it is another great one. One day I got a call from her and she said, "What are you doing next week-end?" I told her nothing that I couldn't rearrange. Now to K. when she said next week-end she really didn't mean - Saturday and Sunday. It could mean anything, but you knew it meant "for at least three to four days sometime in about a week". So I was up for it, I was game.

The trip was to Roanoke, Virginia and we were driving. Or I should say, we were taking my car and I was driving. She said, "Oh, we are just going there to see about this ambulance they want to donate." Well, it actually was a fully-equipped ambulance slated to go to Mexico and there were cameras, newspaper people, a speech and all kinds of hoopla. It was pretty amazing.

I told her how great it was and she agreed but then said, "Now we just have to figure out how to get it there."

"We can't drive it there?"

Oh yeah, I remembered - that "crossing the border" thing again. Well, as it turned out about a month or so later it was flown in on a really big plane - *"and that's all I have to say about that"* (Forrest Gump).

People believe many different things and probably will have varied opinions about my miracles. That's okay. I have learned over the years that there are fewer things that are clear - black and white, and more things that are in the "shades of grey".

Many argue over beliefs and religions and who is right and who is wrong. It appears to me that love, peace, kindness, forgiveness and generosity are at the core. Our arguing is all about who said it and what should we call it and call the person who said it.

Who cares?

As for me, I experienced these occurrences as miracles from God. I know K. experienced them slightly different but the end result was the same. It changed our lives and in turn we were there and available to help change the lives of others.

Isn't that what it is all about anyway? Just thinking out loud...

Are you ready to see what happens next?

Well then, follow me through the looking glass and down the rabbit hole.

CHAPTER NINE

"So Life Goes On..."

So, that covers two of the three prejudices; addiction, "they just can't stop" and depression, "they just can't get out of bed". The third prejudice I had to "eat crow" over was abusive relationships, "they just can't get out". I had been in a work-related one but it was over, and I was out of a job. But since the Prozac had done its' job, I was now running on a chemically-balanced full tank of gas.

My relationship with my daughter was improving and life overall was looking brighter. After she gradated high school I made the decision to move to Georgia and get a new start, a geographical cure. I had found a house, a job, married my wonderfully addicted boyfriend, (in a ceremony at a state institution, no less) and moved all my worldly goods. North was about to meet South, or as I like to call it, "my own private civil war".

Before I do some more strolling down Memory Lane, I probably need to talk a little about those early miracles. When they happened they were extremely powerful experiences for me. They let me know that there was a Creator that truly cared about me and my life. They also built up my faith, very valuable these two things and very simplistic.

What I have come to understand over the years and many miracles later, is that *all* miracles are expressions of love. Deeper than that, the real miracle is the love that inspired them. Whether it is a miracle we are receiving from God through someone or a miracle we are giving as God uses us to do so - all are inspired by God's love. I think the miracle is that God still loves us even though we do a very good job of *trying to lose that love, trying to give it away or destroy it.*

Originally created in our Source's perfect image, we have strayed from the original and become a facsimile. Similar to a copy you make at a copy machine, when it's very low on ink. Or trying to make a recipe from memory and you leave out a few key ingredients or adding salt instead of sugar. Ughhh!

And even more amazing than his love, is his faith in us. Believing that after he does the miracle in our life we will pay it forward, pass the miracle along – the way it's supposed to be. Time after time we don't. And time after time we even forget to be grateful. Luckily the "Alpha and the Omega" is patient and in it for the long haul, the eternal plan.

You see another goal of these miracles is to realize God's forgiveness and then pass that on too! Extend forgiveness to others. Usually when we really need a miracle either we have fallen short in some way or made a wrong decision. It could be that someone has hurt us or taken advantage of us. It really doesn't matter because in each situation someone needs forgiveness. The miracle is an outward expression of this need. It's taken me a grey hair or two to grasp that it takes being intentional to look for the miracles because not all of them are show-stoppers. Some are small and delicate, quiet and shy. But we need to live each day devoted to miracles, recognize them and hit the forward button.

"Oh, what a wonderful life" it would be!

That's it, "It's a Wonderful Life" starring Jimmy Stewart as George Bailey. This is my most favorite movie of all time. I cry at the end each time when George's brother flies home in a blizzard and says, "To my brother George, the richest man in town!" George's whole life was about sacrifice and making *someone else's* miracle happen, never realizing how amazing his life had been. "Thanks, Clarence".

Okay, back to the war between the north and the south. The move to South Georgia was a culture shock. I couldn't understand anyone, but it never occurred to me that they couldn't understand me either. Dah!

Everything was so slow. People talked slow. They drove s-l-o-w. They did everything slow. I was still on "Yankee" road-runner mode, and I am sure everyone thought I was the crazy one.

What also took some getting used to was when you met someone or checking out at the grocery store, there was always some personal "How ya doing" conversation that *had* to go on *before* any business transpired. It's a ritual, if you didn't do it, you were rude. It's called "Southern Hospitality". So there was some rudeness coming from me before I realized how to do the "dance".

I had one little fellow say to me in his best long, drawn-out drawl, "We do things a little different down here in G-e-o-r-g-i-a", as I ran my mouth telling him what I thought he should do and how he needed to do it at a NASCAR pace.

Tom joined me and we began our married life. I wish I could say things were blissful. But geographical cures never work. I was still mixing up enabling with love and he was still having one foot in AA, one foot in Teen Challenge and his butt on the fence – and in jail. You know what eventually happens when you straddle a fence too long, you fall off in a pile of horse manure. So we divorced and parted ways, Tom to another sabbatical at a lovely, state-institutional vacation spot and me trying to become a Georgia Peach or Southern Belle, can't remember which one.

Neither really fit.

This was a very confusing time for me. I really believed that Tom and I were supposed to work side-by-side helping people with addictions. It was something that I knew deep inside. What I didn't understand was why it wasn't happening and how clueless both of us were. This is why it took a long "trip around the mulberry bush" for both of us to get straightened out.

He tried to contact me every day via phone or mail, I refused both. I was sticking to my guns, playing hard ball, tough love. I just wrote him one letter. It was my only communication with him over the next year and a half. It was short and not so sweet. Basically it said, "I have nothing to say to you until you graduate Teen Challenge." Years later it was said that I "kicked him to the curb".

Hey, sometimes getting a swift kick and hitting the curb is what a person needs!

I might need to do some explaining for those who don't know what Teen Challenge is. Teen Challenge is a ministry started by David Wilkerson around 1960. It developed into a year-long residential program for individuals (not just teens but adults, too) with life-controlling problems. In essence, a spiritual boot camp which has a 90+% rate for those who complete the program. I had done some fundraising for the Teen Challenge Crisis Center back home and fully believed in its ability to help people overcome addictions.

I now was working for Willingway Hospital, the premier addiction rehabilitation center in the south. And I was introduced to Al-anon. It took all three of these educational experiences for me to begin to understand addiction and how I couldn't control it.

See I am a control freak. You probably guessed this already. I suppose I thought I was magical or something. Us control freaks always believe things like that. Shoot, we can't even control ourselves. How do we think we can control people, places and things? Complete arrogance, I guess.

Wait, I do need to share a quick story with you.

For many years I really didn't like myself very much. There were times when I did, but it always seemed to revolve around how much I weighed or if I was getting positive or negative strokes from the male gender. But, I was working the evening shift at WillingWay on the detox unit when a beautiful woman about 35 years old came in. All the time I was admitting her I was wishing I was her; beautiful, thin, rich, well-dressed and well-spoken - all the things I wished I was. As I was asking her personal questions we got to the part about why she was there. She told me she was a terrible alcoholic and her husband had hidden all the liquor from her so she drank a bottle of perfume for the small percentage of alcohol it had in it.

That stunned me for a second. I had heard stories like this, but hearing it directly and seeing the pain in her face and the tears streaming down her cheeks touched me to the core.

She said she would trade everything she had in the world not to be an alcoholic.

This was a turning point for me.

I realized that I needed to be grateful to be me and not to be wishing to be someone else. Because you never know what is really going on behind closed doors and in other peoples' lives. All we see is the outside, what people want us to see. But until we walk a mile in someone else's shoes, we don't know their pain. And wishing we were them could get us a life much worse than the one we have now.

It also deepened my compassion and made we realize life should be lived each day. Lived fully every day and savored. Don't waste your time worrying about the past, you can't change it and tomorrow hasn't come yet. Learn to be happy exactly where you are!

Savor life like a rich, gooey chocolate fudge brownie. Eat it slow. Don't die wondering what it would have been like to eat that brownie. Play the game of life to the limit, no regrets. The sky's the limit!

If you don't pay close attention you will only see your life as full of problems. But really all those obstacles or challenges are just disguised as problems. Their true purpose is to train you. How else can you learn patience or empathy? How else can you learn to persevere and develop endurance? How else can you become tenacious? It is what makes us who we are and if we learn the trick of making lemonade out of lemons we can relax under a shade tree now and again sipping a tall, icy glass of that tangy brew.

My daughter actually made me realize this. When she was about 23 or so I felt I had to apologize to her for being selfish and putting myself and my needs ahead of being her mother. She told me not to apologize because she was who she was because of it, and she liked who she was. She went on further to say that she felt some of her best qualities came from me and were developed because of what we had gone through.

Wow!

Again, she's still more mature and insightful than me.

So, I decided I was going on with the plan without Tom. I was going to convince the town they needed their own Teen

Challenge center for men. So 40 hours week I worked my regular job and every spare minute, about another 40 hours a week, I worked on trying to open a center. I read, studied, talked to people and visited Teen Challenge centers talking to their directors and staff. I tried to raise awareness and m-o-n-e-y! Both were difficult to accumulate.

Almost everyone I talked to in town didn't think there was a drug problem. It was 1997. Of course there was a drug problem! Statesboro is a college town. Of course there was a drug problem. Maybe I was talking to the wrong people? I tried writing grants. Well, actually they were request letters to foundations and corporations. No response there.

After about six months I was disappointed and exhausted. Then a funny thing happened. A wonderful woman came up to me one Sunday before church and handed me several cassette tapes, yes this is before CD's. She said that God had told her to give them to me. The tapes were by David Wilkerson, the founder of Teen Challenge. It was a three-part series entitled, "Death of a Dream".

I waited till the following Saturday to listen to them. I was on my way to the beach, which was about an hours' drive away. I was so engrossed in what the tapes were saying I got lost and it took me two hours to get there.

Now I knew why she had given me the tapes. In a nutshell: 1) if you think God has given you a vision or assignment to do something, give it back because you could of dreamed it up yourself, 2) don't think about it, talk about it or worry about it. If it's truly his idea, he will give it back to you *the way he wants it* and, 3) if he does, there is a window of opportunity to do it in, not before or not after - or you'll miss it!

Sounds profound, right?

Well, I decided since nothing else was working I would try it. So I totally stopped doing anything, I told myself that I had made it all up. It was my idea and that if God wanted me to do something he was going to have to let me know. And then I did nothing. I just went about my business living the life of a now twice-divorced woman in South Georgia, trying to carve out a life with a pen knife.

I did some minor dating. I went on a short trip with one of my nurse friends and went to the beach every other Saturday. One particularly beautiful day I was driving back from the beach very relaxed and toasty from the sun and sand. The sky was a beautiful shade of blue and there were big, white billowy clouds in the sky. I was listening to music from the 70's, my favorite, when all of a sudden straight ahead of me was a window.

Seriously!

There was a huge paned window in the sky smack dab in the middle of my path.

Immediately I knew - it was my window of opportunity!

Remember I told you I had this simple faith like a child. Well I was still simple and so God had to make sure it was plainly simple, very plain and so big that I couldn't miss it!

Okay, I thought, "Now what?"

The whole drive home ideas, thoughts and possibilities were pouring into my head. I was driving and writing them down at the same time. I didn't want to interrupt the flow of it all.

This process went on for at least 30 minutes. It was going to be a women's center not a men's center and I even had a rough sketch of what it was supposed to look like. I also had the outline of what to do next and where to go to look for the people and resources I would need to make it happen. Actual names of people even popped into my head.

Now, I wasn't sure whether they were brand new to me or ones someone had mentioned and I had forgotten, but they were there, on the list to contact.

I must admit for a while I didn't tell anyone about the window in the sky. I thought, "These people already think I am too far out there, I don't want to scare them off". But like a true plow horse I began to clear the path kicking up a lot of dust along the way. I didn't want to miss that window of opportunity, it might close or disappear. And it was time to shout about and share the miracle!

Things began to happen. A local attorney helped us set up our corporation at no cost, as a donation. And a local CPA helped us set up our 501c3 as a donation, too. His name was one that had been thrown out to me.

There are no consequences, it was a great pitch and we hit a homerun. Gotta love God's baseball team! People started to listen, money trickled in, an advisory board was set up and now all we needed was direction. The direction came in the form of the Florida Regional Director who met with our group.

He told us we had a good start but for us to have a serious chance of opening we needed to raise $35,000.00. Hah! It might as well of been $35,000,000.00. Where were we going to get that much money? We had about $6,000.00 at that time. Six months later, after more meetings, presentations to groups and churches and a banquet we added another $15,000.00. We were getting closer!

But it was still difficult because everyone kept asking, "Where's the building?"

We were at a stalemate. So I contacted the Florida guy and told him my dilemma. He said, "I guess you need to start looking for a building." I was thrilled! A while back I had made friends with a woman who was a real estate agent, so I called her and told her to start looking. She told me there was much to choose from but she was worried that I was going to run into a big problem, zoning. Little did I know zoning wasn't a problem it was Mt. Everest and I was about to become a professional mountain climber!

She found a great property, it looked big enough and the price was not too overwhelming. It was out in the country on about three acres. Who was going to care about us way out there anyway? So now that all of the bases were covered, how were we were going to buy it?

Well, about a week or to earlier I had gotten a small donation from a local businessman.

Whoa, let me back up.

For over a year I had been talking with the pastor of one of the biggest Baptist Churches in town. I had shared with him that I wanted to open a center to help people with addictions. I had asked him if he would allow me to speak directly to his congregation. Since he didn't know me from the woman in the moon, he kept delaying his answer, but would meet with me every few months to monitor my progress.

This he did several times. Then one day he called and said, "I want you to come to our Wednesday evening prayer and I will give you five minutes."

Yippee! I was so excited! I went, and after the service several people came up and encouraged me. One man handed me a check. Later I found out he was a local real estate developer and also owned many rental properties in town.

So, now...

When I didn't know where to get the money I told the realtor I was going to call this man. She looked at me with an odd look and said, "You mean you are just going to call him up and ask him to help you?" "Yup, I 'm gonna do it just like that."

I called and he agreed to meet with me the next day. Now, I was nervous. A little voice just kept saying, "Just go." So I did. I showed him a picture of the house and described everything about it. I did a lot of rambling, I mean I rambled on and on and on. Finally he looked me square in the eye and said, "What do you want me to do?" I was so bad at asking he had to practically do it for me.

"Can you help us get it?" I asked.

"Yes!"

Just like that, just "Yes!"

That was enough for me. We set a time the next day for him to look at the property. He was more "construction-wise" then I and he thought it looked sound and with a "thumb's up" we were off to the next step. Unfortunately the next step involved the dreaded "z" word, *zoning*.

Now my realtor was still in a state of shock, but she felt confident that this property being away from town should be easy to get adjusted. Now that's a funny word, "adjusted". What that really meant was re-zoned. Unlike a fun z-word like zebra, zoning is not fun or pleasant. But I hadn't found that out yet. So, naively we put up our notice informing the neighborhood we wanted an "adjustment" and it would be discussed at the next zoning meeting. No problem.

In talking with our businessman donor he suggested I work on getting a small group of sympathetic individuals together who would be willing to help in this endeavor, but he did agree to be the "lead dog". You know, like in an Alaskan dog-sledding team. A team with a lead dog, all equally matched and running together, pushing forward, pulling the sled and it's rider across the great tundra.

Great picture, isn't it? These sled dog teams are crucial to survival and my team was going to be no different. They were going to be crucial to the survival of keeping the dream alive, the dream of making this all happen.

Okay, I had the lead dog, but now I had to find the rest of the dogs - the perfectly balanced team. And, I needed to do it quick since the zoning meeting was only ten days away!

I failed to mention earlier that after that day driving home from the beach when I saw the big window in the sky something else started happening. A networking loop began to emerge. You see, for over a year and a half I had been all around town talking to and meeting people. It's a relatively small town so sometimes one loop would intersect with another loop and in that intersection, in that cross-section, BINGO! A sled dog would appear.

So I began to round up the dogs. I had a handful now, not quite enough but I was getting close. Everything was falling into place, or so I thought.

The evening of the zoning meeting arrived. My realtor, the businessman, my pastor and I were there. I had never gone to a zoning meeting before and I was a little nervous. They talked about a number of projects and several people presented their cases. I was glad we were going to present last, because I was able to pick up some helpful hints. Then it was my turn. I got up and began to speak. I had roughly ten minutes to plead my case. I think I did a good job, at least that's what they told me.

Unfortunately, I was not prepared for what happened next. It was now open for discussion and the opposition's turn. I guess I assumed there wouldn't be any. Fatal error!

One by one the neighbors got up and proceeded to raise outraged voices and spew all the potential horrors of letting drug addicts live next door to families, families with innocent children. How one of the women might escape and break in their home and rob them or even worse. They were loud, firm and united. As it goes with zoning boards, the decision rests with the majority. And this board was not going to go against the neighborhood, no matter how worthwhile the cause was.

There was no rebuttal time for me to say, *"Hey you already have these individuals in your neighborhoods in active addiction, often having to resort to crime to feed that addiction. They need treatment and it's safer to have them in a supervised program rather than causing chaos on the streets."*

The members of the zoning were kind and had smiling faces, but my answer was "No". I was crestfallen. People came up to me with condolences like I was a family member at a funeral. And I guess I was. At least it felt like that.

There was one last option open to us - to take it in front of the county commissioners. But I was getting the thumbs down from my pastor. His belief was that the door had closed and he didn't understand why I would want to be in a neighborhood where the people obviously didn't want me or the ladies we were trying to help. I remember talking to people out in the parking lot and the next thing I knew from down deep somewhere in my stomach or heart (I know it was one of those vital organs), I heard the words, "See it through".

Well then. Was I going to have an experience like Kevin Costner in "The Field of Dreams", "Build it and he will come?" I didn't have a cornfield to knock down but it did seem like I had a field of obstacles that needed flattened.

Next stop - the county commissioners.

100

I made appointments to meet with each one, all wonderful local businessmen who took time out of their busy schedules to listen. They all assured me they saw the value and the need, but again, in a democracy there are two sides. I realized I must be making some waves when I got the first nasty call, it was the first of many. And they got nastier and nastier as it got closer and closer to the board meeting. Ugly would be closer to the truth.

Of my supporters almost everyone was 100% on board. The other few were just waiting in the wings to see what would happen. Then I got this bright idea. It exploded in my head like fireworks, brilliant! What occurred to me was: that addiction is a disability and with the ADA, we *couldn't* be discriminated against!

Slam dunk, a three-pointer! We win the game!

I called the State, talked to several attorneys and learned a lot. I was right we couldn't be discriminated against!

They sent me the regulations and I went to work constructing my speech, like a master builder erecting a skyscraper. I let a few people in on my surprise strategy. I think they were amazed I thought of it and was going to do it. But disappointedly, they didn't seem as enthusiastic as me. I don't know why not, it was a Perry Mason move, "The Case of The 40+ Yankee Woman". I wrote my speech on note cards and practiced and practiced.

The night finally arrived. This time I had more supporters with me as I entered the meeting room. I walked through the doors, "Boy! Was there a lot of people!" I mean really, it was standing room only. But I was prepared. I was loaded for bear, as the saying goes. They called out my name. I stood and walked to the front of the room. I remember it so vividly like it was yesterday even though it's now more than 15 years later. I can still see their faces, all those eyes fixed on me and what I was about to say. I introduced myself and in great excitement and anticipation I glanced down at my index cards, I was about to dazzle them.

The cards were blank. What?!

Not only were the cards blank but my mind was blank also. I frantically turned the cards over a few times – nothing. I started to sweat (or perspire as they say in the south), ladies don't sweat.

Oh, contrare!

Sweat was pouring out of me. I only had ten minutes, I had to say something. And I did, but I have no idea what I said. My mouth was moving and there were words coming out of it, that's all I remember. Then I sat down.

My supporters all were saying, "Great job!" "Better than the last time!" But my ears were buzzing so loud I could barely hear what they were saying.

I blew it!

I had it all planned. I had researched and studied and agonized over every word I was going to say. I was going to tell them they were discriminating against these women and it was illegal and I had the laws to prove it. I was going to be magnificent! But instead, total failure.

I couldn't believe it! I had written those cards myself. I had them in my purse and then in my hand. No one could have gotten to them. I had checked them right before I stood up. Was Harry Houdini or Merlin back from the grave and messing with me? Was David Copperfield in the audience?

I glanced down at the cards in my lap and there in my own handwriting were all the fancy and factual words I was going to use to state my case and win the argument.

Was I crazy? Had I lost my mind?

I didn't have time to think it through because now all the neighbors who were legitimately a little crazy were getting up and saying all those nasty things again.

If fact, it was getting so ugly the county commissioners started to feel sorry for me. I could see the sympathy in their eyes. And they were starting to get annoyed with all the flaming darts and arrows being hurled at me.

Finally, it was over. Thank God!

Of course, the neighborhood won and there would be no Teen Challenge center on that property – ever! My supporters kept telling me what a great job I did and they were happy and of course, disappointed, but still happy.

I didn't get it. I was embarrassed, dejected and basically demoralized. Maybe I shouldn't have done this. What did it prove? What good did it do? I could almost hear my pastor's voice in my head telling me not to do it.

Then a funny thing happened, one by one three different county commissioners came up to me. The first one told me not to worry that I'd find a property and then proceeded to tell me about a grant opportunity with the county and the phone number of who to contact. Over the next few years we would receive tens of thousands of dollars through that grant.

The second commissioner came up to me and was very encouraging. He pledged his personal support and so did the third commissioner. Both men were instrumental in helping us over the years raise money and in finding resources to finance the center.

Then I got it!

The "seeing it through" was not to get the house. The "seeing it through" was to give these individuals the opportunity to be touched and the opportunity to be active partners with us in the ministry. Without going through it all they would have missed their blessing of "blessing us". Pretty heavy stuff! Building my character, courage, endurance and credibility, building the supporter base and getting a lot of publicity was just the extra stuff we gained, the icing on the cake.

Now let's talk about those index cards.

Maybe "seeing it through" and "not seeing" the writing on the index cards was God's way of being ironical. How about, "I was blind and now I see." This was now the second time an intervention to "my senses" had been done to steer me in the right direction. A pattern was starting to appear. But in all truth, I believe it was his way of stopping me from making the biggest mistake I could have made. *How did I think I was going to get the support of the very people I was going to accuse of being prejudice and of discriminating?*

Was I an idiot?

Just because I was right doesn't make it right.

Or better still, doesn't make it smart.

Being right isn't the key - doing the right thing is.

I learned a lot that night about me and about God. And I decided right then maybe I better try to stay out of the way and let someone else be in charge of this cruise ship. *I think he's the better captain!*

When I think about this now, I can see it all makes sense and falls perfectly in line with what I have been reading about, the law of attraction.

We have to attract into our life what we want through thought and action.

But to do this, to attract what we really need and what is going to benefit us most in making our life abundant and fulfilled - *we need to be attracted to God.*

Letting God attract us and in turn, us attracting God, is for me - the true *"law of attraction".*

Oh, and by the way...

That house would have been too small. It was in the wrong place. It would have been a disaster, a gigantic mistake. It was the wrong one, the wrong house.

The right one had been staring us in the face all along...

ONLY THEN

They say love makes us aware of "who" we are,
Is that true?
They say it makes us more aware of ourselves.
Aware of what, what we have or what we lack?
Our flaws and shortcomings,
Or our greatness?
Of our neediness,
Or of our strength?
Maybe it's our nose or our teeth,
Or maybe our hair, or lack of it.
But who are they to say who we are?
I say maybe the truth is found in loving yourself,
Only then can you truly know who you are.
                                    – Susan Farah

CHAPTER TEN

"So I Can't Believe It!"

Still reeling from what had happened, I decided to try to take a few days and clear my mind. Let the *"worrying of how we were going to find a property where no one would care if we were there"* go for a few days.

So, to get a better perspective I made a gratitude list. Gratitude lists are pretty cool and it usually does a good job of taking my mind off my problems. I made up my mind I would write down the "top ten" things I was grateful for:

1) I had a job

2) I could pay my bills

3) I had several good friends

4) My daughter was in graduate school and doing well

5) I had my health

6) I still had a lot of supporters and growing support

7) I had God

8) My parents health was good for their age

9) Tom was now in a Teen Challenge program

10) I was able to come up with 9 things

Well, really I had a lot to be grateful for!

For quite a while now I had prayed for the ability to see people as God sees them. Not only was that prayer answered but, on occasion, I was able to feel their pain. The first time this happened was with Tom. I think that was part of the strong connection we had. Not only did we have the same spiritual beliefs and a strong emotional bond, but I was able to see through his mask. You know, that mask, that tough outer shell we use to protect ourselves – well, he had really tough one!

You know, maybe this ability to know or feel what another person feels is what happens with a lot of us when we feel a special connection with someone. If so, then there must be a reason. Why else would we be able to do it? Just for the heck of it or the fun of it? I don't think so. Usually it's not too fun.

A few days later my cell phone rang and the businessman was on the other end. He said, "Ya know, I just realized I know of a house that might work. Why don't you go take a look at it?" He said this very nonchalantly like; "I'm gonna take out the trash." When he gave me the address I was startled, I passed this house everyday! It never got my attention.

It was almost 100 years old, really big and right on Main Street. But it was barely visible behind the overgrown bushes and trees. Originally it has been a beautiful southern Victorian family home with a wrap around porch. But over the years and through the hands of various owners, it had been battered and bruised. Along the way it had been renovated into small store-front businesses and most recently, into apartments. I was told that during the times it lay vacant it had served as a dry place out of the rain for the homeless and the crack addicts. Great!

Again, how ironic.

The current owners were developers, apartment rental men, quite common in a college town. They had been trying to fix up the place but were running out of money. There were several people renting rooms there now, somehow that was hard for me to believe considering the shape it was in, but it was true.

We walked in, there were holes in the walls and very rickety electrical wires stapled to the walls. It had those very old windows with the pulleys, most of them broken. You could hear the wind whistling a tune as it passed through.

What was the tune? I don't know. Maybe, "Whistle While You Work" or "Cry Me A River". But it was big, had five bathrooms and plenty of rooms to make into bedrooms. Most of the backyard was a parking lot and there was a small carriage house. Yes, this house was so old that it had a carriage house, which we could use for a chapel.

It was perfect! This was the center.

And, you will never guess where it was. It was next to the county commissioners building, where we had our zoning meeting. Imagine that! It had been there all along just waiting for us. It had been there when we talked to the zoning board. It had been there when we talked to the county commissioners. We just didn't see it. It wasn't time. But now was the time.

Maybe that was another one of those "not seeing" and then "seeing" occurrences.

Hmmm...?

Now, here come the obstacles. The buyers had to want to sell it at a low price. I had to get all those sled dogs running in the right direction, they held the purse strings. And, oh yes, lest I forget - z-o-n-i-n-g!

Oops! Let's back up. There are no obstacles, right? There are only opportunities.

Well, I think I heard quite a few opportunities knocking. I think a few rang the door bell, too. It's a funny thing that I learned from all of this; when you are in the flow, on the right path – things just happen. So here's what happened...

The sellers sold the house to us at a low price and were able to take advantage of a tax write-off, since we were a non-profit. And remember that "see it through", well since this property was on Main Street, in the business district the zoning was "no problem". In fact the city was thrilled we were going to take over that property since it had been *nefarious*. My only problem now was how the actual purchase going to take place? *What about the money?*

There were a number of meetings and a lot of talking, but we still only had a few supporters who were actually willing to step up. We were stalled and almost out of gas! We needed one of those miracles.

Wait, I am having a flashback! It is stopping me from proceeding so I must need to share it. The flashback is something that happened years ago when I first met Tom. One night about 3 am I got a phone call from him.

"Please help, come and get me", he pleaded. So I got dressed and snuck out of the house where my daughter was sound asleep.

I drove to the "projects" and somehow found the corner where I was to pick him up. I shut off my headlights and coasted to a stop. This may sound crazy but the only thought that ran through my head was not of getting hurt or killed but of the cops arresting me and it would be all over the newspapers and I would lose my job.

Crazy, huh?

So, I waited and I saw him slowly stagger to the passenger side of the car. As he was opening the door I realized that someone was also opening my car door. It was a menacing looking man and he was trying to get in!

With the prowess of a tiger I kicked him in the chest with my foot, grabbed my door while at the same grabbing Tom by the shirt and pulling him in the car. As I did all of this I stepped on the gas as hard as I could and bolted down the street with his door still hanging open and him, halfway in and half-way out.

Somehow we made it out of the projects that night. Looking back I had to be out of my mind! I would never attempt to do that today. Well, maybe I would if it was my daughter who was in trouble. But back then I was younger and fearless or maybe just "senseless".

Since I am doing this remembering I am reminded of a speech my daughter asked me to give at her high school National Honor Society induction ceremony. I had been cleaning out some old boxes a few weeks ago and came across the speech I wrote. Again, I felt fearless back then. Here are some of the excerpts:

When you look in the mirror, what do you see? Do you see a person who wants to succeed? Not afraid to take responsibility and ready to make some tough choices? It is up to you and you alone what you see in that mirror because you are what you think and believe you are. If you expect nothing from yourself then that is exactly what you will get – nothing. But if you expect much from yourself and others, you will get much.

Have the self-confidence not to turn down opportunities. Don't be afraid to except challenges, what is the worst thing that can happen? You will fail? So What! SUCCESS is built on "Re-defined Failures".

Let me say that again: SUCCESS IS BUILT ON RE-DEFINED FAILURES.

Think about that, *success is built on failure. So, you can't fail. You may have failed, but, you can't fail. Period...*

All of us have potential, areas of potential and possibilities. We owe it to ourselves to take it to the limit! We have a responsibility to make the most of our potential, to make the most of what we are and what we have. If we don't, we have left a big void. We have left the void where the person we were meant to be is supposed to be. We have let ourselves down. We have let others down. We have let the world down, because what we do and say, and we what do not do and do not say affect others. We shape the lives of others, so we have an obligation to make a difference. It's our duty. We weren't put here just to accumulate stuff.

<u>*We are the stuff that things are made of!*</u>

And how do we succeed no matter what? You first succeed in your mind. If you see it, if you feel it - it will be real.

I heard a wonderful story about an American Olympic track runner, Prefontaine. He ran every race in his head before the race started. Every step, every turn and curve of the track - every inch of it. Not only did he see it in his mind but he felt it, every bit of it. How it felt as his shoes hit the track, the wind rushing past him, the stretching of his muscles and the muscle burn he felt as he pushed toward the finish line. All in his head, before he even walked on to the track.

If we can just do what he did, see and feel ourselves walking up to the platform and receiving our Master's Degree or standing up in front of a classroom of students teaching or in that hospital operating room suiting-up before performing surgery. Once we have done that, the real thing is just a repeat performance.

We have already done it! We have already succeeded.

And you know what else I remembered?

I had encouraged and made a difference in someone's life, Mary. Mary had an interesting life, as a young woman in the 40's she was a beautiful nightclub singer. She met a very worldly man much older than she and fell in love. They eventually married and she gave up her career and had seven children. Those first ten or so years were exciting and financially great, he was a powerful man. But after a while the power was gone and he had not saved for the future so their later years were hard. He died when she was in her 50's, he was almost 80.

She had a lot of unrealized dreams but she was one not to do a "woe is me". She chose to talk about and remember the good times. She always said she was lucky because she had the finer things in life. She had lived a blessed life and been at the top. She didn't talk about the bottom. She wasn't a "bottom feeder", or a bottom "lifer".

It was an extreme privilege to be in Mary's life during her last years. She had many health problems and couldn't get around easily but she was an inspiration and an encourager to me. I was lucky to have the opportunity to do something to repay her for her kindnesses.

Mary wrote songs and poems, she had all her life. She also had written music to several of them. I was able to put her creations together in a little book and have about 30 copies made, so she could give them out to family and friends. It was just a simple thing, but it was recognition of her life's work as an artist. One of her songs was performed in a local production at the Playhouse Theater in our town for the 4th of July. It was a patriotic song, Mary was very patriotic and a woman of strong faith.

She was thrilled!

She got all dressed up and on opening night she sat in the front row and received a beautiful bouquet of red roses. When they announced her name, she stood up. It was as if she was a young girl again for those few hours. Afterwards, I took her and a small group of friends out for drinks at a fancy restaurant. That night it was like old times for her, when anything was possible.

I guess I had these flashbacks to remind me to remember. Remember why I am here. Remember my purpose. Remember what I am really capable of doing because what I was about to do, I was going to need the courage to know anything was possible!

So here goes. Where was I? Oh yes, Not enough money and supporters to buy the property.

By this time four or five people were basically interested, but not one "declaration of independence" signer on the bottom line yet.

Then there was Mr. C. Now for the last year or so I had been paying for a small office space in a little building on Main St. It was just big enough for a desk, a few chairs and a phone, but it was a start. This had been my base of operation. It was $125 a month and I had been paying for it out of my paycheck. It was my contribution to the cause.

The owner of the building was Mr. C. He was in his 70's and very much a southern gentleman. He had an office in the building too and about once a week I would see him and say, "Hi". Occasionally we would talk and he would ask me how my project was coming and what new things, people or ideas were up and coming. After awhile he told me about his wife who was ill. We had some long discussions about her care and medications, pulling on my nursing background. During this process I had come to find out he was one of the most beloved men in town and on the board of directors of one of the local banks. I had been hoping that he would agree to be in my group of supporters but, although he had been always helpful and very interested in what I was doing, he had declined to get directly involved.

I summoned up the courage once again to talk with him and poured my heart out. I told him about the house and where we were at so far. This time he agreed to meet with the group. And now with his support, the other two individuals I was hoping would join - did. Mr. C had been the key.

So now we had seven prominent local supporters who were willing to sign the note at the bank. We had no mortgage, the supporters would be paying the interest on the loan once a year for the first few years until we could get the mortgage on our own. Oh, by the way it was Mr. C.'s bank.

Yoowho!

We were officially Teen Challenge of Statesboro, Georgia. And we had a center!

So now what? Did I forget to mention that all along I thought that my job was just to get this thing up and ready so someone else could take over and run it?

Again, this was another one of those denial scenarios. Because if I would have known the real deal, that I was going to be the director, running the program and raising all the money and responsible for all the students - I wouldn't have done it. I wouldn't have had the nerve. I was intimidated by the thought of running a ministry, I wasn't "spiritual" enough or holy enough or *something enough*.

So now I am thinking, "Great! I need to call the Florida man." Well by the end of the conversation I realized this thing was a lot bigger than I thought and it was going to be in my life for a while longer. Again, it came through the back door.

The next crazy thing happened about a week later. I went into work, my boss called me in his office and he yelled at me. This was highly unusual. He had never done that before. In fact, I don't know if he ever yelled at any employee before.

He told me the "Teen Challenge" thing was too much and that "I was going to have to choose, "WIllingway or it!"

So without hesitation I said "Teen Challenge!". I walked out of his office realizing I had just given my notice and was without a paying job. Oh, my God!

Again there was the call to the Florida man. And that is how I became the paid Executive Director of the program. Unfortunately the pay was very low, so low in fact, that I couldn't afford my apartment and eat too. It was a good thing the house we had just purchased had a small empty apartment because it was to be my home for the next year.

Now, the funny ending to this little story...

The next day when I went in to work my boss was sweet as pie again, like the day before didn't happen. He even wished me well with the center.

I realized that it hadn't been him asking me to choose. It had been someone else asking me through my boss, *to choose*.

I guess I made the right choice...

CHAPTER ELEVEN

"So How Much Is This Going To Cost?"

So, what happened next you ask?

Well, we had to get the current renters out. This included a girl with several cats which she never allowed to leave the apartment. The stench was unbearable not to mention there was an inch of grease on the kitchen floor, I almost fell flat on my bottom! She literally had never cleaned that apartment in the two years she lived there. There were piles of clothes and junk mail everywhere, she had made paths between the stuff just to be able to walk from room to room.

Then there was the one occupied by several fellows. Let's say they were uniquely and brightly dressed individuals of the night. The apartment was not too bad really. The next apartment was pretty well kept by a woman who worked locally the only problem was when she left she turned off the electricity and didn't tell me - leaving the freezer full of meat which began to rot and attract maggots. No matter how many times we cleaned it we couldn't get rid of the smell! Then I was living in apartment #4. The other two large apartments were upstairs and vacant. They were vacant because they were unlivable for humans!

What to do first? I put an ad in the paper for volunteers to help clean and with some individuals from church we had several Saturday clean-up days.

We cut down the bushes which revealed the potential of a beautiful Victorian southern 4,000 square-foot house. That's if you could look past the rotten wood and peeling paint. The roof was a little rough, it had been leaking in several places for a long time and would need major repair. Once the renters were out and we had gotten rid of all the trash, drug paraphernalia and critters, we were ready.

Ready? Now that is a deceptive word. It usually means that you can proceed and everything is in place. It is a positive word, giving off some really great vibes. Well, my "ready" was not giving out any warm "fuzzies". My ready just meant the un-professionals had done all they could without professional help. This place was going to need $150,000.00 of work at least. And then, furnish and outfit it for the women who would make it their home for the next year of their life.

I did know one thing I needed, a builder's permit. So I went to City Hall to get one. They were nice. in fact the gentleman who gave it to me was great. The first thing he said to me was, "You know you have a serious fire trap over there." Very comforting words I might say. But I got my permit and proudly posted it on the front window.

The next Saturday among the volunteers was a carpenter and a builder. I was really excited! They both gave me a full day of back-breaking work. At the end of the day I asked them both if either could commit to helping me. The builder sincerely said he would like to but he had already donated his time that year to help build a Habitat House and couldn't do any more. The carpenter, who I later I was to find out was really a *destroyer of wood* not a builder of wood, agreed to help. So we planned that the next Saturday would officially be the day we would start remodeling.

You see, we had to take all those apartments and make them into one big house again. There had to be bedrooms and bathrooms, a classroom, a central kitchen, a large dining room plus a large living room. In addition, we needed an office area with space for pastoral counseling and mentoring.

So Saturday came and it went. It went because this carpenter that I thought was a blessing took a sledge hammer and knocked a huge hole in the wall that was the only thing holding up part of the house *and then* admitted he didn't know what he was doing.

No kidding! Now he tells me. Now what do I do?

God and I had a long, long talk. Well, mostly I talked and he listened.

And then I waited...It was my turn to listen because I needed an answer. A big one!

It was quiet. In fact, it was quiet for about a week. During this time I still was going about town trying to talk to anyone who would listen about our needs. It was slow going. I talked to Mr. C. As always he was patient and kind and just said, "The answer will come". I had a hard time with this. I was still a typical Yankee, always in a hurry, I had no patience.

Oh, I forgot to tell you. Awhile back I had prayed for patience because I knew that was a weak area of mine. Bad timing don't you think?

Better watch what you pray for because you usually get it at the most inconvenient time and in the most inconvenient way!

Finally an answer came. But again it was; "see it through". Where had I heard that one before? Oh, yeah, when we went after the wrong house. I didn't get it. What did it mean now?

See, that's the other thing we humans need to learn the hard way, the *"what does it mean part"*. Because if we interpret it wrong we can waste time and energy doing it wrong before we figure out what it really means and then do it right. From this you realize Susan has spent a lot of time going round and round.

Okay, after thinking and talking to my self for about three days the only answer I could come up with was that "see it through" meant to ask the master builder again. So I found his number and summoned up the courage to make the call. I told him I knew he had already said he couldn't help but I whined, *"We have been trying with to it with volunteers and had just put a big gaping hole in the bearing wall. And please was there anyway he could help?"*

There was no hesitation on the other end of the line. He immediately said, "Okay. I'll see you on Monday." Obviously neither of us knew it yet but God had already prepared his heart and was just waiting for me to make the call.

You know this is an important lesson and I need to take a minute to talk to you about it. What if I hadn't made the call? What if I hadn't taken the time to try to figure out what "see it through" meant? What if I stopped at, "I've already asked him once and he said no?"

The bottom line is - *what if I hadn't done my part?*

God had already done his. He prepared the man's heart but I had to do my part and physically make the call. This is a crucial point, that is why so often things don't work out for us. We are waiting for some miraculous, earth-shattering thing to fall into our lap because we think that is the only way it is from God.

No, this is not so!

There is always – *a-l-w-a-y-s* – the part that we are supposed to do.

You see, there is a two-way covenant going on. Whatever the need is, whatever we have asked and prayed for; *there is God's part and there is our part*. God will wait a long time until we do our part. Remember: *He invented patience,* he has the patent on it. We just need to work on having some.

I was thrilled!

It was Wednesday so I only had a few days to wait. Monday morning came and he walked in with two of his carpenters. He said, "Okay this is the deal, I will donate my time but you will have to pay my two helpers here $10.00 an hour and they get paid at the end of every week. We will stay until the job is done".

It was perfect! This center was going to be done right. It didn't matter that we didn't have enough money to do it, **yet.** It didn't matter that it was going to be harder to remodel the whole thing rather than build a new building. God had decided to use the most unlikely person; me a short blonde Yankee woman who had just moved into town two years earlier and who was not a natural-born citizen of this South Georgia town. Not to mention everyone now that I was going to need to get to help this vision become a reality was going to be a new acquaintance. None of that mattered. It didn't matter because I was oblivious of those facts. And in this case, ignorance was bliss. So I was very blissful!

He then rattled off about ten questions: Had I contacted the fire department? What were the specifications for the ramp? Did I realize that we would need new wiring, new plumbing and new windows? Did I realize the fireplaces were falling in? What were the specifications for the working kitchen? Had I contacted an architect since so much was needed to be done?

Had anyone looked at the roof? Was I going to need a sprinkler system? And the list went on and on. He needed to know all this stuff before he could start to rebuild, do he wouldn't have to remodel what he had just rebuilt.

Whew!

So, this is the story...

I had already noticed that there was an architectural firm on Main Street just a few blocks from the house. The next day I stopped in and asked the girl at the window if I could talk with an architect, there were actually two who owned the firm. B. came out to talk with me. I told him what we wanted to do and all about Teen Challenge and then emphasized the "non-profit" part. He said he didn't' have much time but he could do something rough, maybe it would be enough to pass inspection.

Oh, yes, I forgot to mention, every step of the way we were going to have to pass city and county inspections. He called a young man out from the back of the office and told him to follow me over to the house, take some measurements and get a list of the types of rooms we would need to have.

Architects have always had a special place in my heart. When I was in high school I was never really good at art, but the area that I excelled in was design. Once I realized this I was hooked. I used to buy home design books and pour over all the floor plans and dream about building the houses. I was a closet architect and now I was even more in awe of them.

They were going to help me pass inspection!

And, B. didn't just do a rough little drawing, he did incredible professional architectural plans that I know were worth thousands of dollars. B. was a part of us now, and later he became a board member.

I had so many things to do and find out about I really didn't know what to do first. I must admit that I had a unique, or more honestly, an unorthodox way of deciding. I got out the phone book, closed my eyes, starting praying and then plopped my finger down and whatever was under my finger was the name of the company to call. And this was how God, not I, decided who was going to be a part of this project.

The realization was - not just anyone was supposed to be a part of it. This place was very *special*. It was special because the women, who would be coming there, these hurting women, were very special to God.

I think this is the place where I need to share an unusual phenomenon I had experienced in church several times with you. It would always start with me feeling an overwhelming urge to walk up to the altar. The first time this happened I was so nervous that I stayed in my seat until I couldn't stand it any longer.

I went up and knelt down, surprising the pastor as it wasn't the specified time to do this. I began to sob uncontrollably. The thought of all the people who were trapped, in the chain of addiction, flooded over me. Then a fierce pain that started in my gut and made its way to my throat hit me. Lastly an extreme heaviness, like a lead shield, smothered me - all I could do was weep.

This was the burden. Not my burden, but God's for his lost children. So these were the beloved ones that would be coming to our center to have their lives transformed and to be loved and encouraged. There was no room for error now. It wasn't about me anymore.

My finger said I better contact the fire marshal which, as it turned out, was precisely the next step. Yes, emergency lights, a fire alarm system and a sprinkler system were now on the list of the things we needed and had no money for. At the same time, it was important to line up the electrical and plumbing contractors since what they would be were doing would be under what others would be doing.

Again, with the finger... And again, *the miracles came!*

Everyone I contacted agreed to donate all the supplies and equipment, we just needed to pay for the labor. This ended up being a miracle in it's self as these workers would drop in after their other jobs were done, never taking away from the stability of the companies and their committed projects. And because of this we literally paid pennies on the dollar for this work. Next we found a sprinkler company from Savannah, who even though had just finished a Habitat House, agreed and said, "Okay, I can and I will do it."

My days consisted of the contractor showing up every morning and giving me a list of nails, screws, lengths of wood, gadgets, hinges and others things that he needed, "Right now!" And I would scramble to Lowe's or Walmart's or someone's truck to get them. And at the end of each week money would go out for the helpers. It was a constant stream of running and paying and fund raising and asking and begging and finger pointing from morning till night.

I would hear the hammers and buzz saws in my sleep. I also would smell all those fumes and breathe in all that dust since I was living right in the middle of all of it. Then there were the endless questions about what to do here and what to do there and what did I want.

This is a funny side story about the contractor and me. He used to drive me crazy with some of the questions, one in particular was beginning to get on my nerves. I would think, "Why can't he remember?" We already went over this about three or four times. He had no trouble remembering the other ones we discussed. After about the fourth time this happened I realized what he was doing. When he asked me a question and he *liked* the answer, he would just make it happen. He would just go on and do it. But when he didn't agree or like what I wanted to do, he wouldn't say anything but a few days later he would ask me again. And ask it like he had never asked me before.

It took the "sliding wooden doors" incident for me to figure this out.

There were these awesome wooden sliding doors built right into the wall between the living and the dining rooms. They were so cool! They were old of course, put in when the house was originally built. I loved them. I wanted to keep them. After about the eighth time Mr. Contractor asked me about them and for the eighth time I said I wanted to keep them, I stopped and turned around and said, "You keep asking me because you think I am wrong, right?" He smiled a sheepish smile and nodded his head. So the next thing I knew the doors were lying on the front lawn. And from that point on I saved both of us a lot of aggravation and started asking him what *he* would do if he were me.

We were moving right along, day after day and week after week. Things were beginning to take shape and then, we ran out of money. I mean I saw it coming, but I thought something would surely happen to either slow down the bleeding or sweeten the pot.

Neither of those things happened.

I had found some brick to close-up the fireplaces and some beautiful pink ceramic tile for the hallway and foyer. They practically were giving it away but we would need a skilled workman to lay it. I needed $500.00, I didn't have $500.00. In fact, I didn't have $50.00! And in a few days there would be a week's wages due our carpenters.

My finger was on the phone to call and cancel everything when something made me stop. There it was again, "See it through". Oh man! I can't pay the people I already owe and now, I am supposed to order some more work to be done?

Again, "See it through". Now I was really feeling like Kevin Costner when he heard, *"Go the distance"*.

I guess sometimes you have to think big and stop thinking small. This was the time for me, I couldn't worry about what others thought about it - this meant my board. Because by this time I did have that board of supporters (funders) which turned into my board of directors and they knew the puny size of our bank account and yet the work was still going full blast.

It's kind of like a politician or president of the United States, no matter what you do half the people won't like it and won't agree with you. But if it works out then all of a sudden everyone was on your side all along. I was really hoping God had something spectacular up his sleeve because I was going to need it!

It didn't happen that day, or the next...

Something I need to get off my chest here. I have always believed that criticism is not about "you", it's about the person who is doing the criticizing. It's been a struggle for me, but I try hard not to criticize others. However, it has bothered me for a long time how people can think it is okay for others to live poorly. Or that underprivileged people, people who are struggling or those who have made bad choices should have to live from the scraps of others and then - *"be thrilled about it."*

Jesus ministered not just to the sick, blind and lame but to the prostitutes, murderers and tax collectors. He sat down and ate with them and not just a piece of moldy bread or rotten fruit but the best that was there!

Since he is the example, why do people think that people with addictions are less than? I have never understood this.

When the burden was burned in my soul to make a way and make a difference in the lives of these hurting women; women who had sold their bodies and hocked their mothers jewelry for crack and heroin, God didn't say, "Make them live in a hell hole because they deserve it." Shoot if we all got was we deserved in life, we'd all live in a hell hole! We all have messed up, hurt people and done wrong. We just didn't end up on the evening news, in the newspaper or in jail for them. That's my philosophy.

That's my philosophy!

I have been to places where people were trying to get their lives straightened out and get sober, hold down a job, get their health back and reconcile with their family. They were trying to do this in a drug-infested neighborhood because that's the only place that was available to them. The furniture smelled like rotting potatoes and had holes in it with the springs hanging out. But that is all that was affordable for them. And they had to eat, well I am not sure what is was, but I couldn't eat it or even describe it.

Now, I ask you, "How can someone feel loved, be confident and look at themselves worthy of sobriety if people keep reminding them every second that they are in this dung heap because of the mistakes they made?"

How?

Remember this verse from the Bible? *"If you do it to the least of them you do it unto me."* That just doesn't mean the good stuff you are doing, that means the not so good stuff too!

That is why I knew that the center had to be beautiful. Because God sees all of us as beautiful and these women

126

needed to know that! The community needed to know that and all that walked through the doors of our center needed to know that - to see it, to feel it. Feel the love and feel the respect.

How can you teach people to respect themselves and to respect others if the people who they are told to respect don't respect *them* enough to offer them what everyone else wants and has? Please don't let this next example be you:

One day someone knocked on our door and handed me a bag full of clothing. Technically it was clothing. mostly underwear. Well, it used to be underwear, and now it was used underwear. It was so old and nasty with holes in it that I threw it in the trash. I wouldn't even let anyone else see it.

I was furious!

I wanted to run after the car and say, "Why didn't you just throw this stuff away?" Gross underwear, that has to be the worst! I fumed for quite a while then, my anger changed to sadness. I was sad because that person thought it was okay. Think about what I just said. **They really thought it was okay.** *They not only thought it was, "okay" for someone else to wear "what they wouldn't", but actually thought that they were doing them a favor!*

So sad...

The only thing those pieces of cloth should be used for was cleaning up dirt and they were even too disgusting for that. But maybe that was the way that person thought of these women. And if she thought of these women this way then down deep she must think of *herself that way, too.* And the only way she could feel better about herself was to make sure in her mind there was someone lower than her, low enough to deserve trash.

So please, don't be this person. If you feel that tug on your heart to donate and give something to someone else, "Make it beautiful". Make it worthy. because it wasn't you who planted that thought in your head it was from above *and he's not into giving out trash!*

So, I have now just stepped down from my soapbox and I am done lecturing for today, thank you very much.

You have probably already guessed that I took very special care in how, who, what, when and where donations came from for this very special place. I wanted to make sure the women felt cared about and knew the importance of taking care of themselves and the beautiful things that had been provided to them. You see that was the secret, the key to unlock the cure. It was a principle they had to learn.

But, I am getting ahead of myself now. Let's go back to where I left off. Where were we? Oh yeah, in the middle of remodeling.

Like I said, *"We had no money."*

I had heard some whispers about not making it so perfect or about cutting corners, but as I just shared, this was not an option. So, all I could do was move forward and hold my breath.

The little fella came to do the brick and ceramic work. It was going to take him three to five days to complete the work. Since God had his time table and I had my window of opportunity, maybe it was time they intersected.

Two days later a $500.00 donation came in from an anonymous donor. I still don't know who it came from. The next day the contractor saw the strained look on my face and asked, "Do you see that church across the street?" It was the First Baptist Church and we were directly across the street from it. "I am a deacon there and several of the men who have donated to you are also. In fact, the big guy (the lead sled dog) is the head deacon. Why don't you go ask them for money?"

Out of the mouths of babes, or in this case, a sawdust and dirt-covered genius!

But I must admit I was nervous. It wasn't the first time in my life I was nervous but this time was different. I called up the big guy and asked him. He was quiet for about a minute then said I would need to come to the next meeting which was in a few days and present it to the group. He also said he would be supportive but couldn't persuade anyone, the group would have to make the decision.

I agonized over what to wear, how to fix my hair, and how much make-up I should put on. And that was the easy part! What was I going to say? I know what I wanted to say, "HELP!" But the key was; what *should* I say?

The evening came and I walked across the street. I felt small and intimidated, I really needed to snap out of it. I couldn't go in there and make a fool out of myself. Then that little voice inside my head said, *"Hello, this isn't about you!"*

Oh yeah, it wasn't. It wasn't about me at all. I felt better, not taller or less intimidated, but better.

Again, I don't remember what I actually said. I know I reminded them about what we were trying to do, how much we had done so far and that the contractor and "the big fella" were already playing a major part in it. And, we needed money or else we couldn't complete it. But as to the details, I don't remember. I was done and I left.

There were no fanfares or pats on the back at this meeting. Just, I was done. I had to wait. There is that waiting thing again. I hate that. I have always hated waiting. Waiting in the dentist office or the doctor's office, waiting in line at the bank, waiting in line at the grocery store and being on hold on the telephone, I hated it all.

Philippians 4:19 ran through my head and a peace came over me. I knew somehow God was going to supply all my needs, all our needs. Then the belief grew stronger, I remembered that God had painted me a picture of how it was going to be. How lives would be changed and all the differences that would be made in people's lives.

I realized that not only was it not all about me, but that this hadn't been *my* idea to start with. So there really wasn't anything to fear. My job was to keep going. *Just keep going.* It was God's job to bring what was needed.

Sounds real brave now that I am writing about it years later. But at the time it didn't feel so brave or so great. But I had done all that I could do.

Now it was time to wait...

CHAPTER TWELVE

"So We Are So Close..."

Two things happened simultaneously.

I got a call and an invitation, first the call. The telephone rang and on the other end was the pastor of the First Baptist Church. He said he would be right over, which wasn't hard because he was just across the street. I was hoping he had a check, a big one.

Over the last few years I had met with him often and he was always sincerely interested in how the progress was coming. When the doorbell rang the first thing I saw when I opened the door was a big white envelope. I hardly noticed the hand holding the envelope or the man attached to that hand. He was talking and I know my ears heard him but the only thing I could think about was what was in that envelope. The urge to grab and tear into it was almost too much to bear. The suspense was killing me!

I smiled and pretended I was caring about what he was saying, but I was faking it.

After what seemed like an eternity, he handed me the envelope and asked me to open it. Honestly, I think I was already opening it before he got all the words out. I stared down at the check. It was for $25,000.00!

I don't know if you can call a check beautiful but this one was gorgeous! I loved everything about it, especially all the zeros. I wanted to grab him and give him a big kiss, but instead I gushed and gave him a hug and thanked him again and again. Then he said something very special to me. He was to repeat this little story to a large group of his parishioners some time later, but on this early spring day it made me take pause and realize how far we had come. His story went like this:

"As pastor of a fairly large church I get a lot of calls from people from my church and those outside of my church. They all have something in common, the people on the other end of the line want to meet with me and talk about something they believe God has put on their heart to do. I have met with many people over the years and they have had many great and wonderful ideas. All the ideas have been worthwhile and many of these people have asked for money or some kind of church support. Very few ideas amount to anything, it is an extremely rare occasion when someone actually follows through and the idea turns into a reality."

"Susan, you are an exception to this rule. Every few months you would call and want to meet with me. You never gave up, even though you didn't get any financial support from the church, you kept calling and updating me. You didn't stop until your vision turned into a reality."

I must admit I got a little choked up, this really was a compliment coming from this man. Again it was encouragement from above. Encouragement is so important. I don't care who you are, how old you are or what you are trying to do – without encouragement the human spirit dies. It thirsts and starves for it and without it, the will that is so delicately connected to God's spirit dries up and blows away; like a dried-up, dead leaf.

But on this day my spirit was soaring!

We had the money we needed to finish the renovations. I popped that check in the bank so fast it even made *my* head spin. We needed to be very wise in spending it, there was still so much to be done!

The next project would be to replace *all* the windows except for the two beautiful beveled-glass ones. The rest with their ropes and pulleys, broken glass and wind whistling through them were "outta here!"

We had been haggling with the local lumber company for several months. Since there were over two dozens windows it was going to be very expensive. They didn't want to come down on the price and I couldn't find anyone anywhere who would. My finger had gotten a real work out over these windows.

I sat down and had a little conversation out loud to myself and God, I said, *"Look here, I am basically stingy with this money. Just because we now have some in the bank doesn't mean I want to spend it. Everyone else has helped so there is no reason why so-and-so can't help too. So listen, I am going to make this call now and I expect these people to have changed their minds and sell us these windows cheap enough so we can afford to buy them. So there!"*

Looking around to see if anyone had been watching or listening I dialed the number. So and so answered and I went into my, "I really need your help" speech. I don't know if it was because I had worn him down, he was tired of me calling or if God hit him upside the head but this time he said okay. It wasn't an excited okay, "I am so glad you called and I want to help you so much!" It was more like, "Oh – k... I hope I never have to talk to this lady again, so I'll give in and she will go away and never bother me again" okay.

But this was "okay" by me because I just wanted the windows as cheap as I could get them. And guess what? When the windows came in, it ended up being another funny story.

It was probably the most frustrated I ever saw Mr. Contractor get. In fact after about two hours he left and didn't come back until his men finished installing them. As he left he looked back and said, "Don't tell anyone it was me who put in these windows".

Why you ask was he so frustrated? Well, since the house was at least 100 years old and had been through a lot over the years, it was crooked. I mean everything was crooked. Everything was off, unlevel and at a slant. I don't' know if it was because of all the years of settling and warping from dampness or if the original builder had been hitting the moonshine a little too much - but if you wanted a good laugh you just had to come over and take a look at the windows. They were crooked too!

Another funny story, my girlfriend's husband came over to hang wallpaper in the foyer. He prided himself in doing flawless jobs. Boy, did he have to do an attitude adjustment when it came to this job. He wanted to rip down the wallpaper and almost did before I stopped him. I grabbed his hand and told him to first measure the walls and the floor. When he was done he just shook his head, he couldn't figure out how something could so far off and still be standing. After he was done I thought it looked wonderful. But he said, "Please don't tell anyone it was me who put this up". I just laughed. *Men - they are all the same.* It probably didn't help that I had gotten wallpaper with rows and rows of little flowers on it.

I think this probably is a good place to mention the miracles about the paint, wallpaper and colors. With a house over 4,000 square feet needing painting inside and out, a second building needing painting inside and out, plus a lot of wall paper and border to make it look feminine and pretty – it could have been very expensive. But since my name was: Susan *"no money"* or *"don't want to spend no money"* Farah, we needed to do it cheap.

A volunteer who had showed up for one of the Saturday work parties was the manager of the local Sherwin Williams Paint store. She was a great friend and very supportive of recovery and of ministry. What she did for us was absolutely amazing! Every time some one came in to buy paint and had to have it mixed special and it didn't turn out right or the person didn't want it, the store was stuck with it. So, to get it off their inventory, she would call me and I would come over. I took it all for $.50 or $1.00 for a five gallon bucket. Then every few weeks she would have a sale on wallpaper and border. Again old inventory, odds and ends or rejects I was able to get for a song, I bought them all!

And you will never guess what else happened, everything matched. The paint either was a color that looked great or we created a gorgeous color by mixing it all together. And the scraps and odd remnants of wallpaper and border matched perfectly too! It couldn't have been more perfect if you had been trying to match it.

There are no coincidences, just another gift from God.

I had just put up the border in the living room. It was very Early-American looking with burgundy, navy blue and dark green flowers, of course. It really was the right touch with the cappuccino colored walls. I heard a knock at the door and two men were standing on the front porch with a big sofa and wanted to know if I wanted it. Of course! I wanted anything that was free and not crawling on all fours. *"Bring it in - we never turn down a piece of furniture."*

135

Now remember I just got done telling you about the border, guess what color the sofa was? Yup, you guessed it - burgundy, dark green and navy blue flowers on an off-white background, just like the border.

I couldn't believe it! But what happened next is almost as powerful as my miracle Teddi dog story. It's one that has to be told and shared.

About ten minutes after the sofa was set in place and I was still shaking my head in amazement, one of the workers came up to me with a brown paper bag. He handed it to me and said, "This was lying on the back porch steps". In the bag was a beautiful brass sconce with three candle holders. And in the bottom of the bag were three candles. And what colors were the candles?

Burgundy, dark green and dark blue, I started crying.

I was still crying as I hung the sconce. I stepped back and looked at it all. I could never have matched it any better even if I had had all the money in the world to spend. It was matched to perfection. And the miracle was that someone did pick it out and match it perfectly. The one who knew exactly what would be perfect and wanted to make sure it was, down to the candles - because he can.

And because he was watching over me with Teddi and he still was watching (and still is), and every so often shoots me a little reminder to let me know he is still there. I did remember. Every day when I walked into that living room and saw the sofa and the border and the candles I whispered a little, *"Thank you"*.

Remember I told you it was very important which people were involved with the center. Here's a story that demonstrates why.

The painting of these two houses inside and out was a huge job and getting volunteers to do it really wasn't an option. Between all the remodeling and the very old walls inside and out, the prep work alone was overwhelming. It was a brutal job. How was it going to get done? The materials were one thing and we had that covered, but who was going to actually do the job?

A few months before the "sofa and candle miracle" I had been thinking about Al. Now Al was someone I had met through Tom at several recovery meetings. Al was a painter, but Al had a bad addition problem and I hadn't heard from him in a while. I found out where he was living and went to see him. He was actually doing very well but financially struggling. So, I made him a proposition; we would work around his schedule of meetings and band rehearsals if he could do the painting at a "*v-e-r-y, v-e-r-y*" good price. It was a win-win situation as I saw it, and luckily he saw it that way too, and said yes.

Al was there almost everyday and making good progress though it was going to take months to get it all done. Finally we were down to the last week or so, just the finishing touches inside and the big front porch were left to do. But then Al didn't show up for a few days.

At first I didn't think too much of it. When he got back he said he had been sick which sounded logical. Then a few days later the big ladder and a few tools were missing, they had to be left outside on the back side of the house. So saying that someone had stolen them could be a logical excuse. I went and got another big ladder. Then the small electric saw was gone. Al started to say that it too, must have been stolen when I stopped him.

I am blonde but I am not dumb. Al was in trouble. I called one of the men from the church he was attending and we did an intervention. We called his two daughters and finally they convinced him he needed to go to Teen Challenge. I made a call to the Florida guy and the next day Al was on his way.

We had referred a student and our program wasn't even open yet!

And a year later Al graduated that program. He had struggled for over 20 years with a drug addiction and tried numerous programs but never was able to maintain sobriety for very long. What I have found working and living with individuals addicted to drugs and alcohol - it isn't about not drinking or not drugging; *it's about a life change and a heart change.*

It's also about dealing with the past, forgiving yourself and others and applying and living out solid principles on a daily basis. I believe Al was supposed to paint our center so we would be there to help him when he needed us. We tough-loved him and he made a good choice and continued to believe in himself and in the God who loves him. It's a good story. And I am also glad to say that those carpenters grudgingly agreed to finish where Al left off with the painting. It got finished but those guys really needed to stick to carpentry, painting was not in their skill set.

There are so many stories of what happened during that time, I have forgotten many of them. Every day incredible things were happening, take the two furniture stores who practically furnished the whole center. Both were locally-owned and, since we were a non-profit, they were able to get a tax deduction from what they donated.

But what they did was truly miraculous! All brand new sturdy solid wooden bunk beds, a beautiful new cherry dining room set (two tables with sixteen chairs) and a china cabinet, upholstered living room chairs to match the sofa, end tables and lamps. Also they donated a large entertainment center and large curio cabinet because of some scratches and small dents that you couldn't' even see! A dark brown magic marker works wonders to hide those little imperfections. Lucky for us it was better for them to donate rather than sending it back to the factory. It was like that, a piece of furniture would just show up and we never turned it away.

You don't realize how much is needed to open a residential center. But think about it - 15 people living in a house, daily having to cook, eat, clean, sleep, sit down and study.

Needing to fully equip a classroom for them to learn and study in. Not to mention the office area with office machines, supplies, desks and chairs and food and a van and, well... the list goes on and on and on.

Most days it was overwhelming and that's when the church ladies started showing up. They had bathroom, kitchen and bedroom showers; gifts of sheets, towels, kitchen appliances, utensils and classroom supplies started showing up. It took months but the closets and drawers were full - blankets and comforters, pots and plans, glasses, plates and cups - box after box, a steady stream made its way into the center.

Some days I would just walk around stunned and in awe. I was glad I didn't know what I was doing because it sure was working out better than if I did. I don't know if it was the fact that people felt sorry for me or what, but I know that giving is contagious. And what we had going on was contagiousness. So, I wasn't about to interrupt it. But there were still a couple big ticket items that we needed, couldn't afford and probably wouldn't get donated.

One was a copier for the office and the other was a freezer. David and his men and built us a large pantry out of the side porch. With feeding that many people three meals a day and snacks we were going to need a lot of storage space.

I was asked to go to Savannah to speak to a church one evening, I went. There were only a few people in attendance so the pastor didn't take up a donation for us. I was feeling disappointed and was walking out when suddenly a lady stopped me and thanked me for coming. She said, "I really want to help, what can I do?" She was dressed very plain and in no way looked like she could afford much, but before I knew what I was saying I said, "Well we really need a freezer".

Without hesitation she said she wanted to buy us one and was going to Sears the next day to do it. She took down the address and went her merry way.

Going to my car I thought, "That was a waste of time, that lady is never going to pay $1,000.00 for a freezer."

I've since learned never say "never" to God. Because don't you know, a week later a freezer showed up with our name on it delivered by a Sears truck from the lady in Savannah. I didn't even know her name, I had to call the church to track her down so we could thank her.

Another lesson learned: it doesn't matter what *you think*, just show up and be available, God just needs a body. God can use whoever he wants, whenever he wants and however he wants to do it. He just chooses to do it through us.

A suggestion to everyone - journal, get a journaling notebook or just a pad of paper and start writing. Write down what is happening in your life. Write down the happy, the exciting and the things that make you sad or angry. Do this not just to remember, but to understand your life and to deal with your emotions. So many times we have things running through our heads, but it's usually the aggravating things that get stuck up there and play over and over in our mind. We can't get rid of them or shut them off. How come it can't be like that for the good things - getting stuck on the good memories and walking around with a smile on our face all the time instead of a frown or a fierce scowl?

Write down all that negative stuff that's in your head because by getting it physically down on paper there is a release and a freedom. Then a month, six months or a year later come back and read what you wrote. See how your life is different. Do you feel the same way now? If so, you need to do some hard work. If not, that's great! This is encouragement of how you are winning the battle or playing the game of your life. It also is confirmation and validation of how you are creating your life.

We are all creative beings, responsible for how we are creating our life. So at the end of every day before you go to sleep, think about it. How did your creation turn out today? Was the day what you hoped it would be?

For me, since no matter what I do and say I am creating my life for that day, I choose to create it with color and vibrancy, something that will last beyond just one day. I want to create something I can be proud of and that is in spirit with God, something that is for the greater good of others. Even if that something is to share a mistake I made, a trial I went through or just saying a simple, "thank you".

We don't have to go to a world famous art museum to stare at paintings that past artists have created. Stand back and look at your life and if you can't stand in awe of what you have created *then change what you are creating!*"

Only you can change it. *We are not victims or puppets - but we can act like them if we so choose.*

Ah hah! There's that word again, choose. Remember, we have the power to choose.

I think I read about that somewhere, right?

The gift to choose, use it wisely. If you do - you will feed your true self, your authentic self - your oneness with God. And don't forget to shine, let that light pour out through you. Others will see and feel it. Then they will want it too and want to share it.

It's contagious!

Pretty soon the whole world will be brighter. Now wouldn't that be a great place to live!

This little light of mine
I'm going let it shine
Let it shine. Let it shine. Let it shine...

Okay, so now then let's get back to the copier.

I think it was my Sherwin Williams friend who mentioned a name to me, the name of a woman who worked for IKON. She didn't know what she did or if she could help but it was a name. I called the local office and asked for her, all I could do was to leave a message. About a week later she called me, I told her about the program and what we needed and asked for her help. I really didn't know what to expect this was a big ticket item. As it turned out she was a regional supervisor of sorts and she answered, "I'll see what I can do." I had to leave it at that. I had so many other things to do and try to get donated that honestly, I forgot about it.

A few weeks later there was a message on my voice mail from her. I tried to call her back but we kept missing each other. I was sitting on a folding chair in what would be my office paging through the phone book and poising my finger to start pointing, when there was a knock on the door. What do you think was at the door? A beautiful large office copier accompanied by two delivery men who asked, "Are you Susan?"

I nodded and the one man said, "Here, this is for you." He handed me a hand written note and proceeded to bring in the copier and set it up. The only thing the note said was; "Hope this helps, IKON is donating this to the ministry, you just have to pay a small fee for the copies you make monthly, someone will be contacting you to set up the payment."

The copier was ours free and clear!

Now to rent one of these business copiers would be hundreds a month and to try to purchase one would be thousands. I really was speechless on this one and it takes a lot for me not to have a comment. I kept trying to call her to thank her personally, but I never could reach her. Then the last time I tried calling the person on the other line said, "I don't recognize that name, she doesn't work here".

What?!

Maybe this was a new employee who doesn't know her. Then quickly to my mind came the realization that it could very well be she never did work there. Maybe, just maybe, she was an angel. My angel...

When I talked to my Sherwin Williams buddy and told her what happened she couldn't remember how she had gotten the name, only that when I was telling her how we needed a copier she knew the name and the company. This was a lot like the note cards - now you see it, now you don't. But the result was, it was there all the time. So I chose to believe that copier was there and now was here - and ours.

Someone later did contact me to set up the fee for the copies, she had never heard of that person either. It's just another example of an angel watching over me. It's my choice, and I choose to believe.

I have come to understand then when you are walking "in spirit" or simply on God's wavelength, you do not walk into a new experience or situation alone and unprepared. There has been much work behind the scenes for days, months and even years to prepare the way for you and to pierce the hearts of the people who will help.

Maybe you make a right turn instead of a left and that is where your help is.

Maybe you dial the wrong number and on the other end of the line is your answer, the right answer.

Maybe, you point your finger and it lands in the phone book, you call that number and find out it was the right one to choose.

To me it's like a breath of fresh air, like God has taken a deep breath and blows the problems away. Or in this case, blows the answers towards me. Which ever, I want to be in the path of that wind from God.

And now, this leads me to the second thing that happened, an invitation to a graduation.

So...

CHAPTER THIRTEEN

"So, So Busy…"

The invitation was from my ex-husband. He was graduating Teen Challenge. A few months earlier we had started to correspond under the guidance of the director of his program. He believed as I did that we both were to serve in ministry together. So they geared his time in the program not only to help free him from addiction but to get him ready to be successful in life, and ministry.

I must admit I was nervous. He wasn't graduating until May, a few months off, but I had not seen him in several years. I kept the Florida man updated about all of this and he wasn't exactly pleased. I don't think he even thought we would be able to get the center up and running and have the support to maintain it let alone factor in the addition of an ex-husband Teen Challenge graduate.

I don't think it was in his plan or his wheel-house. His plan was mostly about opening men and adolescent centers. The funding was easier. He often said he really didn't like women residential centers; they were too hard to fund. That was really the last thing on my mind anyway. I just wanted to help those who needed help.

I believe these next scenarios I am going to share are about personalities. I haven't talked about that too much, except mine of course. Which is why I was surprised when I realized that I have always had to deal with difficult personalities. Both my parents had difficult personalities. My dad had a quick temper, no patience and was a workaholic. Does that sound like anyone you know? This was often evened out a little with his generosity to others.

My mom was definitely a martyr, duty-driven and stingy. But she did love her family and would give them anything - if she could control them. Oh yes, mostly she was a control freak and used her illnesses over the years to manipulate my dad. She often tried it with me but my stubbornness usually got in her way. I am sure growing up with them led me to be a difficult personality, too. That part of my self discovery was a little hard to accept. It is always easier to blame everyone else.

I need to pause here, as I was writing this I had to go looking for some old documents in some boxes that were stored away. I hadn't been through them for a few years. I had just thrown them in the boxes with the promise to go through them later. Anyway, since I do not believe in coincidences but that everything happens for a reason, I came across this letter. I had never seen it before.

It was written in poem form and in my mother's handwriting. She had beautiful handwriting, very elegant. I read it and as I did it brought tears to my eyes. Not just because it was something she never told me, but because it made me both sad and mad at her at the same time.

Let me share it with you and then I will share why the "sad and mad". It was entitled:

"To My Grown-up Daughter"

My hands were very busy through the day,
I didn't have time to play games you'd ask me to.
I didn't have much time for you.
I'd wash your clothes. I'd sew and cook,
You'd bring your book and ask to share your fun,
I'd say, "A little later, hon".
I'd tuck you in all safe at night,
Hear your prayers and turn off the light.
Then tiptoe softly to the door,
I wish I could stay a minute more.
For life is short, the years rush past,
No longer is she at your side,
Her precious secrets to confide.
The picture book is put away,
There are no longer games to play.
No goodnight kiss, no prayers to hear,
That all belongs to yesteryear.
My hands once busy, now are still,
The days are long and hard to fill.
I wish I could go back
And do the little things you asked me to.

I don't know when she wrote this. I really don't know if she wrote it herself or had read it somewhere and copied it down. The answer is – **I don't know!** And that's the part that makes me mad.

What makes me sad is that if it was so important to her to write it then is must be how she felt. But she didn't share it. Or she couldn't share it and that is what is so sad. Then I realized it is how I have often felt about my own daughter. I missed a lot of opportunities when she was young to have fun with her, listen to her and make time for her.

Time, it can be a cruel taskmaster.

147

Something else I remembered when I read this poem was all the times my mother would talk to me about wanting to write a book. I believe she was secretly writing things here and there but never sharing them. I realized that this was one of her hidden unfulfilled dreams, one of her yearnings that never had gone away. It was just buried under the weight of fear, duty and insecurity. But again, it also represents the control she had - the need to hold back and know something that no one else knew.

That was the trap, the bondage never to be broken. And that is what is really sad and very poignant. All I can say is "Wow".

Time for the next difficult personality...

My first husband, my daughter's father, was on the surface easy going - but was easily manipulated. And he had a hidden pent-up anger due to his need to be the *good* son and his younger brother, the bad seed, getting all the attention. These dynamics would show their ugly face every holiday, all of which he would ruin. I guess you would say he was passive-aggressive. He too, had anger issues which would rise up and lead us into screaming matches.

For quite a few years I battled with him, You know, who could yell the loudest, each one of us trying to out do the other. My throat would be so sore that I could hardly talk for days. And then one day - I just stopped. I think that was the worst day of all. Because when you are screaming, you are caring.

When you stop screaming, you stop caring.

And that is what happened to me. I gave up. I just couldn't do it anymore. I tuned out, literally. I was there but not there. I guess that would explain the "ex" husband part.

Then of course there was my second husband, Tom. His personality had all the characteristics of the addict but flip the switch and he could be the most generous and sweet person you ever met. He was truly a combination of streetwise and naïve, giving and taking, talking too loud and too much with a brain full of questions and ideas that never shut off. But, would give a homeless person his last dime without thinking twice and valuing loyalty above all else. If he could just get rid of that addiction part, I think you have guessed by now, this is where Susan's need to fix stepped in. Little Miss Fix-it!

The next person I am about to talk about is a newcomer to the list. Even with all my shortcomings I ended up being a pretty good fund raiser and communicator of the needs for the women's center. And I was able to multi-task the purchasing and renovating part of the center. But I really didn't know the essence of the program, the day to day mechanics that was the true miracle of this twelve month discipleship program. So I needed a lot of help. This help came in the way of a woman, a graduate of the program who had been working at a center for the last year. Not only was she all about tough love but she was so detailed; organized and so intentional it would bring tears to your eyes. She could be intimidating and somehow part of her personality resembled my mom's.

It keeps popping up its ugly head!

And to this day I have a hard time with it. I haven't conquered it, whatever "it" is.

So we worked out the logistics and, let's call her BD, came to work for me. She knew it all - the structure, the schedule, the rules and the content of the program. So every day we would start out discussing a few things and then she would spend the rest of the day on the computer. Everything went into neat packets and files and filing cabinets. I could have never done this on my own. It took her nearly two months of constant work to put every piece of the program into place. And in the beginning, we didn't argue or get on each others' nerves - that came later.

Now if BD was going to be the Program Director and I was the Executive Director, we were going to need a full-time, live-in on-duty staff. BD would be doing some of this but the majority would have to be done by that third staff member. Since this program is a 24-hr, seven day a week program minus the sleeping hours, counting up on your fingers you would soon conclude that we didn't work a 40-hour week. Our average weeks were 60-80 hours. We did what we had to do to get it done.

Like Nike. *"Just Do It!"*

So, where were we going to get the third person who would be willing to work these crazy hours? Again, it takes special people to work in these centers - your life ends up being the ministry. There really is no time for an outside life, you have to love the ministry and know 100% that it is what you are supposed to be doing *and* God has put his stamp of approval on it. If not, it turns out bad, real bad!

Luckily we put the word out and there was someone graduating soon from the program and she was interested. And to make sure we covered all the difficult personalities - J. was as different from BD as night and day or oil and water.

Woe is me!

Half the time I had to be the referee between them, but she was available and she had strong convictions about doing what it would take to make it work. She too was a "tough-lover". So I had two staff, both graduates and knew the program inside and out and they also knew what the students would be trying to get away with. This was great for me because back then I was still an enabler.

Yes, it pains me to have to admit to you that I could still be a puppet on a string or a soft touch for a sob story, but it is true. Anyway these were the difficult or dysfunctional personalities I was juggling at the time.

Oh, and of course, there was my personality - I was having to deal with *myself* on a daily basis, too!

This may not be the right time or place to ask this question but "Have you ever seen an angel?"

I have. It's up to you whether you believe this following story or not, but the truth is the truth no matter whether you believe it or not.

Way back when we were still looking for property for the center I had the opportunity to take the day and go to a place right outside of town where we were celebrating our yearly church family day. The place was a private retreat for a local business, was on 50 wooded acres with a 35 acre lake and it was secluded, gorgeous and serene.

I must admit I let my mind wander and envisioned that the corporation who owned this property was going to donate it to us for our center, our center which would be nestled amongst the big shade trees and a glassy-blue lake. This imagining was easy to do and a habit I had cultivated over the years. Sometimes I believed it was creativity at work - seeing it in my head and then when it came true it would be like déjà vu. But sometimes it was just a stress-reliever.

Today I was not sure which one of these methods I was operating in, but it didn't matter, it was fun. Then it was time for the services to begin and we all went inside. The music was exceptionally meaningful to me that night, it was like I was on a different planet. My body felt light as a feather and I was so focused on feeling and experiencing the music I almost didn't see it.

I almost missed it entirely!

It lasted only an instant. It happened so quickly that it's impossible for me to describe in words what I saw, except to say it was an angel. I know that because I just know it in every part of my being. It was a fluttering movement, a flash of light and a physical feeling of breathlessness, awe and calm all at the same time.

There were no flashbulbs or special lighting to explain the light. There were no birds or large flying insects to explain the fluttering. And what I felt I had never felt before and never have again.

I don't remember when the first time I shared the experience was, I know it wasn't that night. It was special and just for me for a long time. I had the feeling that it was a "nudge" or a "you go girl" message. I held it close for a long time until it was time to let it go and encourage someone else.

So that's my angel story, true or my name isn't Susan Chuey Williams Farah.

While back at the center...

Don't think I was being lazy while BD was doing all the office work. I was still running daily on the errands David would send me on, getting what he needed to finish the last of the renovations. All the money needed for everything still had to be found - donated and "fund raised", no local, state or government money did we get. Which meant that daily I was either: 1) on the phone working to get things donated, 2) trying to set up speaking engagements with churches, clubs or individuals, or 3) standing in front of people making a presentation on how they needed to help us.

The first time I was ever in front of a civic group is really a little comical. It was the Lions Club and there were about 20 men. I had my speech on those silly little note cards. When it was my turn to get up and speak I was stiff and nervous, my mouth was dry and what I mean by dry is that I was boring, even to myself. It got worse because the audience was dry, no emotion coming back to me.

When there's no feedback it just makes a bad situation worse. Now I know how a stand-up comic must feel bombing in front of a live audience. Where was Billy Crystal or Eddie Murphy or even Chevy Chase, (wow, that one is dating me) when I needed them? The best part was the questions at the end. Maybe it was because it was almost over and I was relieved or maybe the truth was I was more relaxed and natural. The questions were off the cuff, not preplanned. So what ever came out of my mouth came out and I just had to hope for the best.

Later as I did this more and more I would learn that this latter way of doing things, was the best way. When I was spontaneous is wasn't really me anyway and so things would really start popping and doors and windows would open up. But that night I finally got through it. The good news was they would invite me back the next year and it was through the wonderful Lions Club that many of our ladies would receive the eye glasses they desperately needed. Gotta love those Lions.

Now during these months that BD was getting everything down on paper I was also touring a number of up-and-running Teen Challenge centers. The directors spent time with me and shared their experiences and the pitfalls to look out for. I also observed their daily routines, how the centers looked and how they were set up. I wanted ours to be the best of the best! I wanted to capture the best practices for these special women who would be walking through our doors hoping for their miracle.

The other thing I had to do during this time was to go through the Teen Challenge curriculum, send it in to National Headquarters and become a certified teacher for the personal studies portion of the program. This was time consuming but imperative since I had not gone through the program myself. I had to know what we were teaching and what the students were learning.

I also spent a three-day week-end in a crash course on leading support groups. There are unique dynamics that go on in groups especially groups of dysfunctional people. You have to know "when to hold 'em and when to fold 'em" – like my dad used to say (I think he got that from Kenny Rogers). You have to be able to control the situation without being a tyrant so no one gets runs over or gets left out. And sometimes you have to stop and say "that's enough" - that's the fold 'em part.

If that wasn't enough I was following up on the leads I had gotten from the County Commissioners and meeting with the United Way and the Bulloch County Hospital Authority. And, I was working on the applications for each of them. Whew!

I also had gotten it into my head to write inquiry letters to as many foundations as possible, to ask for start-up money. This idea on the surface proved to be a really big waste of time. However, in years to come, it would prove invaluable to me as a reminder "not to spin my wheels".

It's funny but I think it's really important to waste time on certain things and make a certain amount of mistakes. Some people might think this is a stupid statement. I probably used to be one of them. But that's the luxury of being a "baby-boomer" - we are now in a position to look back and see what was truly beneficial and what wasn't. That's what comes from being an *"experienced in life"* person. And what we call wisdom is often age plus "trial and error". I qualify on both counts.

But alas, United Way turned us down. They did say that the reason they couldn't fund us was that we were not yet serving the community but once we were providing services we would be properly considered. We did get that funding the next year and continued to get it for several years, love that United Way.

Now the Hospital Authority was another story. We made the deadline of the application by one day. And with our recommendation from the city and the County Commissioners we made it to the finalists. At that point I had to make a live presentation to the committee.

Since we had just about used up the $25,000.00 from the Baptist Church on renovations, purchasing items we couldn't get donated and starting to pay a stipend to BD and myself – we really needed this funding. Luckily we had a roof over our heads and no mortgage to pay otherwise I would have been doing this from the street or a homeless shelter.

I was still at the point of being timid at presentations, especially one as important as this. But from somewhere deep inside I heard "Claim your ground", and I did. I envisioned a run-a-way train with my face on it *and* that I could not be stopped. People or circumstance may try to stop or suppress me, but I *would* be successful. The vision would come through somehow.

The committee really did have a lot of questions. In fact, they were quite different from the ones that had been asked before. I guess I gave the right answers because they approved us and the donation was enough to buy all fourteen of the student desks we needed, a desk for the teacher, a study table and 15 office chairs. We also were able to buy a TV with VCR and a cassette tape duplicator (yes, this was back in the olden days before CD's when everyone was still using cassettes).

That tape duplicator really came in handy. As a school we had to provide all the educational and discipleship materials for the women which meant we had to have reference and study books, tapes and videos. Only a small part of this material was from Teen Challenge. All other books, tapes and videos had to be purchased or reproduced. For a solid week we duplicated tapes, BD and I. This was the cheapest way for now, hundreds and hundreds of them. Stories of overcoming adversity, abuse and addictions, we duplicated them all.

Whew! It makes me tired just thinking about it.

Money was trickling in here and there. Some churches were beginning to commit and pledge $50, $100 even $200 a month. Then I got a "yes" from one of my inquiry letters. Union Bank which at the time was connected with Wachovia Bank responded to me. It wasn't with money but something just as good. They were upgrading their computer system and had oodles of obsolete computers to get rid of. *Did we want any?*

Did we want any?

They had just made contact with the "In-kind Donation Queen!"

There was a number to call and so I did. About a week later UPS showed up at the door and basically unloaded their entire truck. Fifteen computers and "the works" - hard drives, monitors and keyboards even down to the mouse's, or is that mice? Computer boxes were everywhere! We stored most of it in the upstairs of the carriage house, since we were not going to be using it initially. But we kept two out for the office. They were nothing fancy but they worked and that's all that mattered.

Everyday was such a blessing for me. And what a blessing to be able to also give back! I know now it's called "paying it forward" and I like that. But back in the year 2000 we just called it blessing someone else. One of the gentlemen who signed on our note was married to an incredibly giving and high-spirited woman. She was always involved in something, I liked that. And boy, she could talk! She could rattle on and on about any subject. I think she at one time had been in the Guinness Book of World Records for "the most hours of nonstop talking" (just kidding). But anyway, they belonged to the Catholic Church and she spear-headed a thrift store for them.

Now it was not a conventional thrift store. I mean it had all donated items in it and people would come and pick out what they wanted, but it was free. *Free!* I loved that. They had lost the space they had been using and he asked me if we could provide them a space. Absolutely! I figured it was the least we could do. So one sunny Saturday morning they set up business in the bottom floor of the carriage house. They even made an eye-catching sign to flag down the drivers-by.

What fun! *It feels good to give back, don't you think?*

We only had a few quirks, thorns in our side, I'd guess you say. A few things we couldn't get around. The company we used for our fire alarm system just wouldn't give us a break. At first I thought they were going to and that is the only reason I picked them but somewhere along the way they changed their minds. Of course it was too late to change companies by that time. Oh, well.

Then there was the electric company. Since we were on Main St. and zoned store-front business, they were charging us at the business rate and it was expensive. We had high ceilings too, so to air-condition it was astronomical! Remember we are now in South Georgia - *hot and humid.*

It was so humid in the summers you could swim in your own sweat!

Oops! Perspiration...

They wouldn't budge, the electric company I mean. It didn't matter that we were a ministry, a non-profit and that we weren't operating a business there. They couldn't change their rules.

Later we found a way to recoup a little of the money. Since we had to pay $6,000.00 for insulation and an air-conditioning unit for the upstairs, we were able to get rebates through the power company. That same company had a foundation and over the years we were able to get several small grants. Yes, Susan "Queen of Asking" let no stone go unturned. But believe it or not, these two were the only negative encounters we had.

By this time we were down to the last of the center's needs. Two local carpet stores gave us carpeting and just charged us for the installation. There was a lot of it too; living room, dining room, office, two large sleeping dorms, the class room and the upper floor sitting area. We put several beautiful ceiling fans in that upper sitting area. Those we had to pay for. I couldn't help it, we needed something striking up there.

But probably the masterpiece of that upper floor was the window. It had been one of the originals in the house. It was huge with intricate paned wedges of beveled glass and when the sun shone through it, it reflected prisms of light in all colors. It was absolutely gorgeous! There was something else special about what was in that sitting room and in the classroom - two murals painted by local young people.

Again as a part of giving back we often would do community outreaches. One we did was to a group of teens representing local schools and churches. It was a special group, high-risk kids. We were always glad to do it. But this time *we* were the ones who were blessed.

About a month after we had done the presentation I got a call from the teacher who said the kids had done a special project for us. They had thought it up themselves, it was their idea and their gift. It was two wall hangings, murals they had painted, each taking up a whole wall. We placed one in the classroom and one in the sitting room. Painted lovingly with vibrant colors that literally came alive and jumped off the canvas! Portraits of women, young and old, their faces smiling and portraits of children - it was the essence of what our center was about. The kids wanted to make sure they were hanging up before our first student arrived, their welcoming gift.

It was like that almost every day. It's hard to put into words how amazing that time was. I know I have spent a lot of time giving details describing the house and everything that went into making it a center, no a home. I guess I've done that to try to convey just how big of a miracle it truly was: *the perfect location and size to meet our needs, no mortgage payment or even interest payments, approval of the city and county, planned out by a talented architect, renovations over-seen by a master builder and furnished for literally pennies on the dollar.*

One day I sat and figured it out and for everything it took to get it from an almost-condemned building to a passing-inspection, fully-functional, totally-beautiful 4000+ square-foot center, cost us $80,000.00 - totally raised through the community. But what was even more astonishing was if we would have had to purchase and pay full price for it all - *it would have been over $250,000.00!*

So...we didn't raise $80,000.00. We raised $250,000.00!

Wait! No I am wrong.

The community *gave* $250,000.00. We just provided them the opportunity to do it.

We didn't stand in the way of *their* blessing.

Imprint on my Soul

I found one today,
That imprint on my soul.
Teeming with vibrancy,
Bursting with brilliance,
Unique to itself,
No other like it.
Holding my breath,
Capturing its beauty,
Away it flew,
Glad to find,
Another soul,
To leave it's remembrance to.
                                    – Susan Farah

A Soft Place to Land

If I give you a part of me
Will you hold it in your soul?
Will you give it from your heart?
If I will,
And you will,
Others will follow.
Together we'll make our cocoon,
A soft refuge, on which to land.
                                    – Susan Farah

CHAPTER FOURTEEN

"So Who's Next?"

I read in "A Course in Miracles" that the truly helpful are God's miracle workers. And our way of praising God is through being helpful to others. That is how we praise him, and as this is happening his love is continuously being poured out. And as more and more of us help through giving and sharing, joy is built throughout the kingdom. Making God's joy complete when this happens.

Can you envision it?

It's like a reverse pyramid. You start out with one or two of the helpful miracle workers helping others, then those they helped in turn help others and so on and so on, until there are so many and the pyramid is so wide that it encompasses the whole earth. Wow, that's a world I would love to live in! How about you?

I have been very fortunate to experience small glimpses into this phenomenon however brief they were, and they have given me encouragement. The encouragement that *we all* can be better than we think we are. We can be kinder and more loving, we can be more generous and forgiving.

Why not?

Why can't we make this world the place that we dream about living in? We have the power. We have the power to choose every day. And every day we make these decisions, these choices - so many choices.

I don't know about you, but it feels like there are two camps in my head. One camp is telling me to do the right thing - be giving, forgiving, kind and full of joy. And the other camp is telling me to ignore the first camp and think of myself first and worry about what I don't have and try to get more of what I do have. Why can't we lock that second camp away? Let's put it in jail, behind bars and throw away the key!

So, today *that* is what I choose to do.

I have experienced the greater good in people and I am not ashamed to talk about it. Am I worried that people will think I am crazy or that I am unrealistic or living on "Cloud 9"? Nope!

Who cares?

At age 59 I think I have earned the right to be a dreamer. And if I can just dream big enough maybe I can help make a difference in this world and just maybe I can help you too. Then I will be one of those helpful miracle workers like in the book.

And then again I think maybe at age of 59 I have earned the right to be wrong.

So... right or wrong, which one?

"Ah, grasshopper, that is the question."

How did you like the way I started off this chapter, pretty philosophical wasn't I? I thought you would appreciate a little diversion at this point. Plus it is a good lead into the next part of the story.

It is now May and time for me to make the drive up to Michigan to attend Tom's graduation. I kept so busy that I really hadn't had a lot of time to think about it. But now it was a reality and I found myself packing my bag and gassing up the car for the long road trip. I hadn't shared with my family where I was going, I didn't know how it was going to turn out. My way of dealing with them was "only tell if you absolutely have to". And even then wait till the last second to do it. I had gathered a boxful of tapes to listen to on the way trying to keep my mind occupied. I printed out the directions and headed down Highway 301.

I had a fifteen hour drive ahead of me and at about minute 33, I was already worrying about what was going to happen when I got there. I couldn't help it. so instead of fighting it any longer I gave in and then made the commitment to give in all the way and do it right. My "Type A" personality came out and decided to do a really good job of worrying and dredging up the past. I got all A's in school, so you know I must really be good at dredging. For the next fourteen hours I watched a series of reruns in my head as I hit that rewind button and let it play...

The first reel playing on the projector brought up the scenes of all the times my parents tried to get me to stop seeing Tom. When they first found out I was dating a *Farah*, I thought both of them would have a heart attack on the spot. My dad even had a police detective sit down with me and tell me all the terrible things Tom's dad, Tom and the rest of his family had done. My dad would have that same detective follow me over the next few years and report back to him when he found me with Tom. They threatened to disown me and write me out of their will. Then it really got ugly, shouting matches and hurtful nasty words.

My mom had a different approach. She tried to kill me with kindness and do things for me, like do my washing or clean my house to "help me out". I even gave her a key to the house. But, what she was really doing was taking messages off my answer machine and going through my mail to see what I was doing and buying. There was no privacy. She was relentless!

One evening she called me on my cell phone and proceeded to fake having chest pains and followed up with telling me how I was killing her. It was masterful but just a little too over the top, since the week before she had tried to fake suicide to get me to stop seeing Tom. I was calm but firm and told her, "If you want to have a heart attack go right ahead I won't stop you, but remember I won't feel guilty because I didn't do it, you did."

She hung up on me and never mentioned it again. She was good at that.

It's a funny thing. If they would have just let it go and not said anything things may have run their course differently. But they tried so hard to stop me, I had to try harder not to let them. It's kinda like reverse psychology, but in a bad way. Parents do it all too often. They can't help it.

It's too bad that children don't come with an owner's manual. I've heard a lot of jokes over the years from great comedians saying, "You have to have a license to drive a car, they should make it a law that you have to have a license to have children."

Wouldn't that be something? You'd have to pass a test. I wonder what kind of questions would be on it? Part of the test could be written and the other part would be a "demonstration back". And who would you get to grade it, Dr. Spock? No, he's dead. How about Dr. Joyce Brothers, I've always liked her. Nope she's dead too.

Maybe... Mr. Spock? Oh well.

Boy wouldn't it be a scream though. Hey, sounds like a great reality show, maybe I should try to sell it to one of the networks. I mean anything goes now-a-days, the dumber the better. Ouch! That wasn't politically correct. I should have said the sillier the better. Oops, my mind wandered off there for a little while. That seems to be happening more and more lately the older I get.

Boy, now there's a reality show for you. I mean it's a *real* reality show, all the stuff that happens to your mind and body as you get older. That's the one I want to sell to the networks. But I better write it down fast because that's another thing that happens to you. Not only does your mind wander off places unknown, it forgets to come home. And it forgets what your mind was wandering or wondering about in the first place!

Okay, where was I? Ha, ha.

Oh yes, movie picture reel #2 in my head. I remembered the night that Tom and I had gone out to a comedy club that his friend owned. We were there for a while having a good time, so when Tom said he had to run to the store for a pack of cigarettes I didn't think much of it. After he had been gone almost an hour I started to get worried and thought, "Where did he go to get those cigarettes, China?"

Then I looked for his friend and he was gone too. By this point I was the last customer left there, it was just me and two employees. I couldn't leave because Tom had taken my car. Oh yeah, I forgot to mention that point. I tried calling him on the cell phone, but there was no answer. It was about 2 a.m. and there was definitely no one I could call to come and get me. Either they were sleeping or I didn't want them to know the predicament I was in. One of the employees clued me in that they had gone out "to get high".

I saw red!

My quick-tempered anger collided with my panicky fear and I started to turn tables and chairs over. I literally turned every table and chair in the place over. I sent table cloths soaring through the air as I unleashed my frustration and vengeance at my stupidity. I don't know who I was madder at - him or myself. Once I calmed down a little the employee, let's call him Jack, convinced me to put everything back the way it was. Then he said he probably knew where they were and offered to drive me to a part of town I had no business being in.

There was my car. He went in and got my keys and brought them out to me. I thanked him and got in my car and drove home. By this time it was 5:30 a.m., there was no time to sleep. I had to leave for work at 7:30 - so I took a shower, drank some coffee and went to work.

I don't know how I survived that time in my life. I was living off alcohol, coffee and chocolate and averaging about three hours of sleep a night. I think the only thing that kept me going was my bottomless barrel of stubbornness. It certainly wasn't intelligence!

Again, it was part of the training I would need to successfully run the center, but what a hell of a way to get it! It would help me to be empathetic with the enablers; the parents, husbands, children and friends, so I could gain their trust and build that relationship. But it also prepared me to be tough on them and let them know what to expect. And not paint a "rosy picture" of how a little band-aide was going to cover a big gaping wound. They needed to know their loved one was going to need an entire body and mind transplant, not a "take two aspirins and see me in the morning" promise or a recovery meeting here and there.

As I let those reels roll by in my head I knew this was the toughest part to reconcile. If I hadn't gone through all of this I wouldn't be doing what I was doing. And what I was doing - was a really great thing. There really isn't anything better than helping others, making a difference in the lives of others. Not just for them, but for the realization you have touched all the lives of the people around them in a positive and miraculous way.

By touching one you have touched dozens maybe hundreds. Or it could be thousands because every year they live "paying it forward" instead of being a menace to society, they are touching more lives for the good.

Hours were racing by as I drove with this balancing act going on in my head. I was bouncing back and forth between the good and the bad times trying to make sense of it all, trying to balance the negative with the positive. I didn't want to make a mistake. I didn't want to be guided by the "Beauty and the Beast" fairy tale scenario or "romance novel" thinking. And especially I didn't want to be influenced by hormones. This was too important. it just wasn't about me any longer.

I stopped to get gas and something to eat. As I usually do I had left early in the morning so I could drive straight through and get there that night. I estimated I was a little over half way there. The traffic was light and the weather good so it was an easy drive. My thoughts started to drift again and a scene popped into my head that made me start to giggle. It was like one of those episodes from "Get Smart". I don't know if you remember or ever heard of that TV show, but it was popular with us "old fogies" back in the day. It was espionage but in a bungling way. Well, that described me and a girlfriend of mine.

We had some funny times together. She was going through some stressful business and personal things and I was divorced and dating Tom, so we would go out to a few up-scale bars and do a little "cruising". It was harmless and hilarious. We were naïve, had married young and had very few, *if any* experiences. So going out like this we thought we were *femme fatales*. We'd get a little tipsy and just laugh our butts off.

She did have this little flirtation thing going on with an older man she knew. Again, it was harmless but since he and his buddy were married, it was like a clip from "Mission Impossible", spy-like. I was the decoy. In other words, if anything happened I would be the one who he was chasing after. This way my girlfriend could be the innocent bystander. We would even do things like switch cars and start off at one location and sneak out to another one just in case anyone was following us.

Silly for grown women I know, but it was the spice in our life at the time. And his wife did actually think something was going on between him and I. So I guess it worked, on her.

I'm not sure what that experience taught me but I've always thought that it was one that I would remember when I was about 90, wrinkled and crinkled and sitting back in my rocking chair rocking away. I would be half senile and half eccentric and I would remember, forget and remember again.

Oh, one thing I did leave out. I did have a secret beau of my own and what I missed out on when I was young I got to play out then, all the way from romantic dinners with Nat King Cole songs playing in the background to leopard silk sheets.

Hmmm...

I had to shake my head pretty hard to get those images out of my head.

The next several hours were spent remembering and balancing. Trying to sort out the truth and what my next steps had to be. All I knew is that I had to take it slow, this had to be on God's terms. Back when I had written Tom in jail and told him we had nothing to talk about until he graduated Teen Challenge was the hardest thing I had every done. And there was only one way that I was able to do it. God had shown me that I was literally killing Tom with my enabling, I was killing him with my love because I was in the way. Instead of turning to God for answers and help, Tom turned to me and I always came up with an answer - and the resources.

I had been playing God and didn't know it!

This really jolted me. But this was the only way I was able to let him go. I couldn't do it for me, even though it was slowly killing me too. So God very vividly showed me Tom's body in a coffin and let me feel all those feelings of pain and loss and then said, "It's because you have become his idol."

What powerful words! But it did the trick. I was able to let go, just barely, and to be strong enough not to give in.

It's funny how we can know what's good for other people but not ourselves, at least that it what I have learned about myself and other enablers. And even though I am no longer a full-blown enabler, I still have to fight it every day.

The truth is - enabling is an addiction. It's an addiction to the person you are enabling.

So, my thoughts kept drifting and landing on some of the good times. No, some great times. I thought about the love, caring, sharing and about the common beliefs and goals we had. How we both wanted to make a difference and use our lives for a higher purpose. I remembered some of the miraculous stories he had shared with me of God's unconditional love for him.

I think it was during this fifteen hour trip I came to the conclusion that God just doesn't use the good or holy people to make an impact in other peoples' lives. He just as often uses the "bad" things that people do. He uses the people who are full of mistakes to teach us and jolt us back unto our path.

Then there was the sign for Muskegon, I was there! It was about midnight, my eyes were blurry and I couldn't wait to lay my head on a pillow, but I was there.

Bbrringg... I opened one eye and hit the snooze button.

"Please, just a few more minutes, okay?"

A few minutes later I rolled out of bed and fixed myself a cup of coffee and ran the itinerary of the next few days through my head. After lunch there would be the visit with Tom. It would be the first time we had seen each other in over two years. Then I would attend the group service at the chapel in the evening. Tomorrow he and I would have lunch with the director and some of his staff and then the graduation ceremony at night. After that I wasn't quite sure, so I decided to spend the rest of the morning in quiet time and prayer.

Okay... so now it's later and I am getting dressed. I had butterflies in my stomach - I was still 100% a girl, so I wanted to look good. I wanted to look so good that he would want to do the right thing for the rest of his life just to have me back. Whoa, little pony slow it down, let's get the bridle on.

Where did all those feelings come from?

Then I realized I really did have a lot of pent-up emotions inside and I was going to have to deal with them. Great!

I took a deep breath, sat down for a minute and started talking to myself, "Okay", I thought, "You can do this".

So, I put on my make-up and got dressed. I must admit I did look pretty darn good without looking sexy. Boy, I thought all of this was in my past and now I have to learn to manage hormones all over again.

During the drive over to the center I tried to keep my mind blank. Now that is a neat trick if you can do it. Trying to concentrate on nothing can be really hard work. I parked the car and went it, I met several staff all of which were very kind and friendly. They led me to the visiting room which doubled as the class room, it was large with a lot of tables and chairs.

It would have to be, the center housed over 100 men. I sat and waited.

My palms were sweaty and I had nothing to wipe them on. "Stop it", I said to myself, "Get a grip".

Then he walked through the door, I had almost forgotten how good he could look. At a quick glance he looked like a young Al Pacino. In fact, when we used to be out together that would happen quite often - the double-take or the "Has anyone ever told you, you look like that actor...?"

My heart actually skipped a beat and I did a little gasp. Those palms were still sweating and now blood was rushing to my head. As he was walking toward me I wondered if I was going to be able to speak intelligently, or speak at all. Then he smiled and I smiled back.

We sat and talked for hours it seemed. We talked about the past, about the future and about the "now". He told me what it had been like for him over the last two years and I shared my life with him. And in all those words my heart that had been so torn apart and so divided against itself was made whole again. The coldness and dryness of it softened and reached all the way to my mind - now renewed, not strained to the breaking point as it had been.

All around me other families talking and laughing and mending their relationships. It was natural. It was perfect. Some may think that you must experience something to know it. Others may think that it falls in the category of "intuition".

For me, knowing is - *knowing*. Knowing just is. And in this way, I knew.

I found myself back at the motel dressing for that evening's service smiling and humming. I realized I had given myself permission to let the past go and not to worry about the future, but to appreciate this moment in time. That night was a wonderful time and experience. And truthfully I was taking it all in because wasn't I just about to open a center myself? And didn't I want to make it the best program I could? So, why not take notes while I was there.

All too soon the night was over and time was pushing with break-neck speed well into lunch the next day. Questions about me, about the center, about the future were suddenly thrown at me. I volleyed, returned the serve and got an ace or two in. It was all good and I quickly understood the love and genuine concern everyone around the table had for Tom and myself. They had just invested a year into his life and wanted to see that new life take root and grow, not just be tossed upon rocky ground.

They wanted him to stay on and do an internship there to help him transition. He had other thoughts. He had already contacted the Florida Teen Challenge headquarters and had been hired to do his internship there. He wanted to be poised to start over and prove he was a different person, ready to tackle ministry.

Passion versus experience; which was right, and which would win?

The graduation ceremony was beautiful and very moving. There were two other men besides Tom graduating so there were family members and friends plus all the students and staff. Each graduate was given time to get up and talk about themselves and what Teen Challenge had done for them. It is a powerful thing to listen to these stories of enslavement to alcohol and drugs and all the consequences they encountered. But this special program and the principles that it is founded on has the ability to change lives from - ones of irresponsibility and chaos to ones of accountability and stability. That is the promise. Many tears were shed that evening but they were not tears of sadness - they were tears of hope.

The next day I was scheduled to leave and go back home. Tom was scheduled to get on a plane and head to Florida. Up until the last second the staff tried to convince him to stay and let them do the transitioning. But he got on the plane and I got in my car ready to get back to the center. That was the only thing I was sure about that, nothing else was that sure.

p.s. I was listening to a tape today and there was a good lesson in it. The man said: *"We can travel in our cars all the way from California to Florida at night with only our headlights shining 200 feet ahead. We don't know what's beyond those 200 feet but as long as we keep our hands on the wheel, our eyes on the road and our lights on - we can make it 200 feet at a time."*

I'll go a foot farther than that.

I think we are not supposed to see any further than that 200 feet, because if we did - *we'd slam on the brakes!*

CHAPTER FIFTEEN

"So Its Only the Beginning..."

Defying the odds, aspiring to be something more, to do something more - that's what I want written on my tombstone. That is how I want to be defined.

If you are what you believe, then whatever you think about and put as the priority in your thoughts and actions is what your life becomes. It is who you are because that is who you have forced yourself to be. This has to be so, there are too many stories of ordinary people doing extraordinary things for it not to be so.

I was watching the Today Show this morning and they were talking about a book coming out entitled, "You Are an Ironman". The story was about a man, who due to cystic fibrosis, would die without a double lung transplant. As he lay there in his bed believing he was dying he thought about all the things he didn't get to do that he had wanted to. On top of this, "Wish list before I die" was to participate in a Triathlon.

Now he was not an athlete. He described himself as "a man with an athlete trapped inside". So, not only did he not die, not only did he get his transplant, not only did he do one triathlon - he has done many! And his story is in the book.

Inspirational? Yes, but it's more than that.

There is a quality that we all are born with. Something so basic and pure it's like breathing. We have just forgotten it - we've forgotten how to do it, how to use it. We have forgotten it's critical to us being "us". It is the essential quality of "knowing that it is impossible to fail", and not only that - but knowing we already possess the ability and the knowledge to overcome *anything*. And we also have the courage to do it!

But why have we forgotten it?

Is forgetting this "it" automatic and happens when we take our first breath and go from "in spirit" to "in the world?" Or is it something that happens over time as the weight and disappointment of the world drowns out the very thing that can help us rise above our adversities? And that all the negative talk swirling around us turns into the negative talk blaring inside our head.

I believe it is the second. You just have to watch little children to see it. To see what they still know and remember, of what we have long forgotten. I don't have a special name for it - a spiritual or scientific name for it. It's just the "beating the odds" quality, the "defying the odds" gene. Everyone starts out with it, but as we mature this gene memory begins to dry up and eventually is gone. And now, somehow we have to fight to get back, we must! The people who can, the people who do - *are the "Ironmen"*.

I, too, want to be an Ironman. That is what this book is about, that is what my life is about. I intend to defy the odds and rediscover that gene. I am going to get this book published and more after that. I am going to devote my life to encouraging individuals to reach their full potential *in spirit* as a personal and leadership empowerment coach.

How am I going to accomplish all this?

I don't know all the "how's" of it yet but:

"I can see the 200 feet in front of me and I can travel that far!"

I know this because I have *remembered* I can do it. That is why it was so critical for me to write this all down. That's why it is critical for everyone, all of us, to do the same, to remember.

Chronicle your life!

Celebrate your life!

Remember who you are! And realize just what an extraordinary accomplishment your life has been!

Remember...

And it's not over yet! You have much to do and much you can do for yourself and others. Get up and get started! Well, finish reading this book first, then do it. No better yet, get out a piece of paper and a pen or pencil.

Seriously, right now I want you to do it. In fact, I am not going to tell you anymore of this story until to get paper and a sharp writing instrument. Okay, use a crayon or magic marker if you have to. I don't care. I'm waiting...

Waiting...waiting...waiting...

Alright, I have to believe that you have gotten out of your chair and are now sitting at the table with the proper tools in front of you. This is what I want you to do. First, I want you to put a title at the top of the paper something like, "My Life Story" or "Everything You Always Wanted to Know about Me but Were Afraid to Ask."

Don't think! Just do it!

Now, write down one thing that you have done that you are really proud of. Something that makes you feel really good about yourself, something extraordinary. Something that you have accomplished or something you have done for someone else that made a difference in their life.

Okay, now you can go back and finish reading my book, you know - the book. The book that I have defied all odds to write and get published.

Hah! See what I mean?

After I wrote this last statement I sat on my back deck which overlooks the Blue Ridge Mountains surrounding Blowing Rock, North Carolina. My backyard is part of the national park and I am blessed to be able to almost reach out and touch the clouds as they nestle themselves between the peaks and valleys. Butterflies, hummingbirds and acres and acres of lush green foliage are my companions. I have one of those very small water features, you know the kind you can buy for $15.00 at Walmarts. But in the quietness you can hear the water trickling over the small pebbles and image it is a gushing waterfall of crystal clear blue water. Relaxing and calming, this alone time eases the worries of the day.

It was then that I was reminded of an important story I need to share. My daughter was dating her future ex-husband who was still in college and an avid sports fan. All sports but especially baseball. He had a dream - his dream was to be an umpire.

I am not sure how long he had this dream, probably since he was very young. He knew everything about baseball and had some friends from his home town who were professional umpires. They had worked with him over the years and encouraged him to try.

His dad had died while he was still a teenager and his mom had raised him. There was not any extra money, he cut grass and worked in restaurants to pay for college. It just so happened that I came into some money and offered him the amount it would take to go to umpire school. He didn't want to take it. But I knew it was important for him to go after his dream. We had several discussions about it and I was finally able to convince him that if he didn't try - he would always regret it. And he definitely was too young to go through his whole life regretting that "one in a million" chance he could have lived his dream.

He attended the camp and did very well. He didn't get the ultimate prize but he came very close. But the important thing is that he took the chance, he tried. He gave it all he had and no matter what, no one and nothing can take that away from him. There would be no grumbling in the back of his head haunting him for the rest of his life of "What could have been" or "You were too scared to try".

There is no failing in life. Even if you don't win first prize - you have won the battle of the "if only" and that my friend, *is a life lived!*

In other words, *"Life is a banquet!"*, thank you Auntie Mame.

What are you waiting for? Go belly up to the buffet table and go back for seconds and thirds!

So, back to the past...

The drive back to the center was different for me. Mostly because - *I don't remember it.* I don't know why exactly, for some reason I didn't think too much or let my mind wander. It was a good thing because I didn't know exactly how the personal part of my life was going to work out and for once I didn't want to conger up a "soap opera" in my head about it. You know how pesky and persistent those daydreams can be, like weeds with prickly thorns growing up amongst your beautiful flowers.

When I got back I was greeted with several tidbits of good news. First of all, we had found a student. Now that may sound funny to you, but the first student you take into your center is critical. They will make or break a center.

We had put the word out for what we were looking for, like an ad in the paper: Female student wanted, must be in the program for at least six months, stable, responsible, good attitude and willing to relocate. How hard could it be?

Well, it turned out it was harder than I thought. We had been looking for several months with no response, but as soon as I hit the door, BD hit me with the news - we had a student!

Over the next month or so there would be details to work out and much paperwork to do. All of a sudden we again had a lot to do in a short period of time. We had been looking at a date in June for the Open House and that had to be confirmed. We had joined the Chamber of Commerce so we coordinated the date with them for the ribbon cutting.

Then there was contacting the mayor and getting a proclamation, this was very important to us. We officially wanted the stamp of approval from our city. We lined up a praise band from a local church and reserved several small tents from local funeral homes. I was keeping my fingers crossed that no one would die right before our opening, we needed those tents.

I had been fortunate to have two doors open for me, one with the local cable station and one with the local radio station, both would be incredible blessings. The cable station would come and interview us at various times and then air it on the cable channel, all to help get the word out. And the radio station also opened their hearts to us and would do free commercials publicizing whatever activity or fund raiser we were doing.

After the open house our cable station even went a step further. They came and filmed our staff and students in action. I worked with the radio station to do the voice-over, my past talk radio training suddenly came in real handy. The station put it all together and came up with a powerful video of the ministry which we used for years. I think they charged us something like $100.00 and would make copies for free as long as we supplied the blank videos.

I can't say enough about the support from our town, our major donors and the guidance from our board of directors. At this point it was exactly what we needed to make the vision a reality. That's another interesting lesson I have learned from experience over the years. God will give you exactly what you need at exactly the right time for what you are supposed to do. All this will go along swimmingly, like clockwork, maybe for years and you will get *real* comfortable, maybe even complacent.

Then when you least expect it - *BAM!*

And what you are supposed to do changes (usually a little *before* you get what you need to make it happen). This will confuse you, it even may scare you. This may make you think you have suddenly fallen out of God's will or fallen out of the sky. Or more accurately, feel like you have fallen into a big, deep, dark well. But after it happens to you a few times, you finally get it. Nothing stays the same, everything changes. Life changes, people change and so must visions, assignments and challenges.

But for now, this was the town, these were the people and this was vision and the time for this special place. I don't want to forget to mention Mr. C. again here. He was always my rock and still is to this day. We still correspond and he is an encourager angel to me.

So, next we had to have a program. Now let's see, we would need an emcee - that would be me. We had the music and food covered but we needed women from a Teen Challenge program to give some testimonies. For this we got students from the center across the state in Columbus. Lastly, our Florida guy would ask for a donation at the end.

What were we missing? There was something gnawing at the back of my mind, but I just couldn't bring it forward enough to see it. Well, it couldn't be that important, right?

The center was full of spit and polish, it was looking grand! We had planted flowers outside and had picked up some used and slightly abused wicker furniture at a yard sale. It is amazing what some white spray paint can do. We hung Boston ferns which made the front of the house with its big southern wrap-a-round porch look like something out of "Gone with the Wind". The only give-a-way as to why it wasn't the mid 1800's was the handicapped ramp. But even that matched the porch, painted white with the same wood-carved railing. *It was perfect!*

People started arriving, speeches and music blared, light bulbs flashed, sweet tea and fresh lemonade started to flow. Many thanks were given out to the donors and board directors, all of whom were there. A special presentation was made to our contractor. I had gotten the idea a few weeks earlier to trick him into coming and then doing something special for him. Even though this man was a tough and rough-talking businessman, he was like a big gooey marshmallow inside. We got him there and he had no idea he was going to be on the agenda. At the appropriate time I brought out a saw that I had gotten engraved with his name, "Master Builder" and our name and date on it. When we called him up to accept his award he was actually blushing - and speechless.

Again, it had been perfect. We couldn't have gotten him anything better.

The mayor was there and presented the proclamation, more light bulbs flashed. The official festivities were about over and we just about ready for the "mingling and true networking" to begin. There was only one special acknowledgement left to make. I've waited to tell you this story because this is the prefect place for it.

Months before when we were trying to find the last person to be part of the group of major donors to sign for the note at the bank, we weren't quite sure who that person was going to be. We knew we needed one more individual so the liability for the rest would be more amiable. Someone gave me the name of a local woman so I called her and she agreed to meet with me.

When we met I took an instant liking to her. But as I started to go into the full explanation of what we were doing she seemed distracted and kept looking around, not really paying attention to what I was saying. Since I didn't want to be rude, I just kept talking and tried to ignore the fact that she was ignoring me.

This went on for about twenty minutes until she finally interrupted me and apologized, "I am sorry if I'm acting a little strange but this was my grandparents' house. It was our family home, my grandfather built it and I was remembering what it used to look like and all the good times we had here".

I couldn't believe it!

Now what were the odds of something like that happening, a zillion to one?

So, for the next hour we walked down memory lane and through each and every room as she told me the history of everyone who had lived there. There had been three fireplaces and unique little nooks and crannies used for hide and seek games and for squirreling away Christmas presents out of the reach of chubby fingers and curious eyes. It was perfect!

What a moving experience for both of us!

She was so happy that her family home was going to be used to help hurting women. Even now as I write this, I realize how important that conversation with her was. After that I looked at the house very differently, it wasn't just a house, *it was someone's home.* It had been built for a family and they had made wonderful memories there.

Wow! After all this time I am still learning and understanding things more fully. Take a lesson from this - never stop striving to know.

Never stop remembering, for it's in the remembering that the deeper truth is revealed to you.

If it's okay with you I need to stop for a few minutes and let this soak in. I'll finish the rest of this later. Thanks...

Okay it's later and I'm back and ready to go on.

Then came the mingling, we gave tours, answered questions and gave out literature. We received several thousand dollars in donations that evening. I was ecstatic but the Florida guy was not, he always expected more, huge sums of money. I don't know whether he really did expect them and was truly disappointed when it didn't happen, or if he just acted that way to keep us always feeling like we were letting him down. But whatever, I was determined not to let things like that bother me - I was unhinged enough most of the time anyway, never feeling like I was holy enough to be doing what I was doing.

Another funny story is about to emerge. Also attending were the many inspectors who had inspected us - you know the group: city inspectors, plumbing and electrical inspectors, fire and water inspectors and building inspectors. I think half the town inspected something in that center. I know the guy from the city just kept walking around and shaking his head. I followed him upstairs and smiled as his words echoed in my ears, *"You know you have an electrical problem up there, it's a fire trap."*

Not anymore, buddy!

But the best one was the local fire marshal. He was great, always helpful and very informative. He seemed to be having a good time and found time to seek me out and ask me when we would be bringing the ladies in. I told him in about a month. He nodded his head and said, "Good, that will give you enough time to get the COO *after* I do my final inspection."

Huh?!

I didn't say "Huh" to him of course, I acted cool as a cucumber and replied, "Yes, our COO". He chatted on, (luckily) and explained that the COO was the Certificate of Occupancy and under no circumstances could anyone other than the paid staff sleep one night under this roof without it.

I was thinking, "Great! It's now 8:00 pm and where am I supposed to put those ten Teen Challenge girls tonight since they can't sleep (under this roof) in the bunk beds in the bedrooms where they already have put all their stuff?"

But I didn't say any of that, I just made the appointment with him the following week for the inspection. He also told me, (again luckily) that he was the one who would be looking for the handicapped parking area, sign and striped parking spaces - which I also had forgotten all about.

Needless to say, we did a lot of scrambling to get all of that ready. Again the city officials waived some, well, whatever they waived it got done. He came - we passed. And in two weeks a small piece of paper about 4 x 6 inches arrived. You would think something that important would have been larger or on special paper or something. But we framed it anyway and stuck in on the wall. We were now official and could occupy, or more accurately - be occupied.

The ribbon cutting and open house had been a huge success, but there had been one thing missing. Have you figured out yet what that one thing was? Did it occur to you as I was rambling on and on?

I'll give you a clue, Florida guy.

No?

Still haven't guessed it yet? Okay, I'll give you another clue, let's make it a game, "What is missing from this picture?" Or more precisely, "*Who* is missing from this picture?"

You ask, "Who could be missing?" "It sounds like everyone in town was there!"

The "who" missing was Tom, he was not allowed to come. In fact, we had to act like we didn't even know each other. There had been no phone calls or correspondence – no contact. Any visits, meetings, letters or phone calls had to be under the strict scrutiny of - yes you guessed it...

"The Florida guy".

Does anyone see a storm brewing in the distance? Do you hear the rumbling of thunder, the flashing of lightening and torrential rains?

Honey, it turned out to be a hurricane with a tornado chaser. But that comes a little later. For now, it was just bittersweet. I think that's the best word to describe it - both wonderful and sad.

I only slept a few hours that night, I think it was something about the bitter sweetness. And just maybe it was the realization that since all of the "*getting ready*" stuff was done so that we would "*be ready*" - it was time to "deliver the goods, deliver the program".

That last part, the delivering the program was something I had never done, it was virgin territory.

That's a pretty interesting word, virgin - untouched, unblemished, pure and in itself just for itself - not for another purpose. I read in a book titled, "The Cloister Walk" that women are very brave critters. We bear creatures that we know are born to die - destined to die. I had not thought about it quite like that before, but what a provocative way to look at it. I sat and stared at those words, not wanting to move on to the next thought, but to stay immersed in that one.

Then another jaw dropper - *everyone comes from a woman's womb.*

Hello, I know it sounds like a stupid statement, but I had never thought about it in the "global sense" before. You know, the thought that maybe it's not just anatomy, maybe there is a deeper agenda going on.

It doesn't matter if you are male or female, if you have a MBA or a DFTLOHK (Degree from the Life of Hard Knocks), if you are a brain surgeon or a homeless beggar on the street or something in between - we all came from some woman's body. It may have been with a sterile slice of a knife and lifted out quietly and gently. Or maybe it was kicking, screaming, crying and messy, either way we all came from the same place, a woman.

Again, making women *brave souls*.

The last thought in this trilogy was that virginity has its existence outside of the "bearing of life and death". This for some reason resonated with me, vibrated not just on a gut level but on a higher soul-touching, soul-searching level, too. And I thought,

"Must we give up our virginity, our virgin territory to bear fruit?"

Hmmm...

The bottom line was, I worried about my future and what the future held for Tom and I. How was I going to be the spiritual leader of this ministry? I was responsible for raising $10,000.00 a month in cash *and* additional "thousands" in in-kind giving, how the heck was I going to accomplish all of that?

I didn't know, since every month we literally would start at zero. What had I signed up for? I guess it was time to raise my prayer life up a notch. Could I squeeze another hour in my day? Maybe if I...

"Oh brother - maybe I just need to stop thinking!"

The next few weeks were a whirlwind of making sure everything was done and in place for our student to arrive. I had already set up rallies in several churches and believed it would be easier to raise money now that we had her. At least I hoped it would be easier to raise money. I had never done anything like this before. But I knew I had to learn the difference between - raising money and donated items for the renovations and start up of the program, and - *raising money and donated items for an existing program.* A program that housed women with addictions for a year and didn't make them go out and get a job, but discipled, mentored and coached them into a new way of life.

Big, and I do mean BIG difference!

I didn't realize it would be a day to day, day after day process of educating and re-educating the public, our donors - and our board. How easily we forget - *how hard it is.*

Then it was July 16th and she was here.

Day 1 – Remember - "Act like you know what you are doing."

And don't forget to breathe!

187

Why I Wrote This Book

I wrote this book for all those people who are like me, who have had questions and have searched for answers - who have always thought there had to be more to life then just their current situation. For all those people who find themselves at 35, 45, 55 or 65 and wondered, "Where did the years go?" And, "Why do I feel like a stranger in a strange land?"

Maybe it's for all those people who try to see the glass half full and not half empty, but are finding it harder and harder to do so.

But just maybe it's because searching for the truth in one's life is like a donut.

A donut, really?

You see, it fills you up but also leaves you empty because it has a hole in it. It's sweet and tasty but lands like a clunk of steel and gives you a stomach ache. And it makes you fat and not in a good way, if there is such a thing as being fat in a good way.

What does all that mean?

You have to take the sweet with the sour. Because without the sour how would you know that something is sweet? Without examining your life how can you find the thread that has been woven very precisely and meticulously through the years to bring you to *this* exact spot at *this* exact time so you can find the answers to all those questions?

The most powerful realization is that the differences between us - make us the same. They unite us. They make us cling to each other like new-born marsupials cling with clenched fists to their mother's bodies, holding on for dear life as she swings through the trees.

Or maybe it's because you are at a place in your life, something reminiscent of where I've been, where you feel alone and totally empty - where God is silent. And because you have been running from yourself and running from life for so long, the only way you will ever stop is to be broken into tiny, little pieces and thrown across the floor like so many slivers of shattered glass. That glass, by the way, is from the mirror reflecting what we see as imperfections, but what God sees as his ultimate perfection – you, just the way he made you, the way he made all of us.

I don't know, I don't have all the answers.

I am not here to tell you how to live your life or what to believe. I am here to suggest and help you explore the possibilities, I am here to share what I have learned and experienced.

It is through experience that we find life. So, this is for you to believe or not. For you to take what speaks to your soul and toss the rest out. I am not here to force you to have the same values as I do or live your life the way I have lived and continue to live mine.

The longer I live the more I realize we argue over the mundane - the unimportant and the meaningless. We *"debate the stupid"*.

Hey, now wouldn't that be a tantalizing reality show, the material would never run out! The debaters would stand in line to get on the show, like on American Idol or The X Factor. And we could get the current presidential candidates to emcee, the ratings would be off the charts!

Have you noticed I tend to use humor to accentuate a point.

I don't know, maybe I wrote this book because there are so many people out there who don't see their life as it really is. They don't see what they have accomplished and how meaningful their life is. They have lost that ability to remember and love *themselves*. They just need a reminder - a little kick in the pants, so to say, to get them back on track. They need their fire rekindled and the flame stoked into a bonfire.

Maybe I am the fire-starter.

So, bring on the heat! Come on get off that couch!

There still is a lot of living to do!

Do you want to hear a good knock-knock joke?

Knock... Knock...

"Who's there?"

"Me".

"Me, who?"

"Me, what is the difference between a blessing and a curse?"

"Ha, ha - okay, I don't know". "What is the difference between a blessing and a curse?"

"Nothing, they are the same".

"How can that be?"

"Ahh, grasshopper... it's all in the eye of the beholder."

I think we live our lives somewhere in between the blessings and the curses. The unfortunate thing is that everything in life is *both*. What blesses you one day may curse you the next and what seems to be cursing you today will turn into a blessing tomorrow. It all depends on the time of day or the day of the week or if you stubbed your toe. Enter my philosophy, *"If you get lemons make lemonade."*

And my friend, if you get a million dollars today, how about giving me some tomorrow?

Okay, so maybe you are in a place of pain, at the crossroads of trying to escape and running towards something invisible and intangible. If that's you, you are not alone. There are so many people today escaping I don't think there is anyone left at home. It isn't just drugs, alcohol or food anymore. You can be addicted to anything. I think most people are addicted to being addicted, finding anything so they can forget about their problems for even one minute.

The internet is a particular sore spot with me. People constantly surfing and tweeting and chirping and whatever else they do. All of us doing this escaping and trying to keep busy so we won't realize how unhappy or unfulfilled we are.

But hey, *"We are supposed to figure that out!"*

We are supposed to sit and think and meditate and let our minds reach a point higher than the top of the refrigerator. It's our job to question and wonder why and why not - and how we can make it better!

So if you are at the crossroads of, "I'm afraid and confused" and "I don't know which way to go" - good! There is still hope for you. You are alive and if you are still alive - there is still hope. And if you believe in "pay it forward" then guess what - *someone somewhere has blessed you and made a difference in your life!*

So it's your duty to figure out your purpose and make the most of it. And you know all that stupid stuff we argue about that builds walls between brothers and sisters and destroys marriages and makes us suspicious of any one different? Well, it's stupid!

I know I am no scholar, philosophical giant, poet or William Shakespeare, but I have come to understand the true teachers over the centuries have all been saying the same thing; we are spirit, we have a purpose and that purpose is love. Simple as that...

If you had to break it down into the twelve words that every great spiritual leader taught, those would be the twelve words. As for me, I know that God is the Great I Am and Jesus is the Christ who died for me. He did it for me and for you and for everyone. But ultimately we all have to choose what we believe. That's the freedom and the gift of "free will". It's free and we can "will" whatever we want, we can be whatever we want. We can believe or have or not have whatever we want. Remember, we are what we believe! And don't let anyone tell you that you are too old or too short.

I have been asked: "What is the book about you are writing?" I have had a hard time explaining. I've sputtered out something about inspiration and encouragement, which is true, but I haven't been able to articulate it to anyone's satisfaction. I think I have realized why it's been so hard for me explain, it's because the book is about "coming of age" and that means something different to everyone. It means something different to everyone who hears it and will mean something different to everyone who reads it. Some may struggle to grasp the meaning because they "came of age" early in their life and there *was no* struggle for them, no confusion, no need to remember.

But we all have to "come of age", all of us.

I am lucky it happened for me at age 59 while I still had time to do something about it - live for it, savor it, eat it deliciously and fully. So, whether you are in your 20's, 30's, 40's, 50's or older; if you haven't "come of age" yet, *you will.* Some may wait until their very last breath and as that last gush of wind fights its way out - they will experience it so clearly, that *last "coming of age"*.

All I know is that, I had to write this book for you, whoever the "you" out there among you might be.

Encourage - Empower - Engage

It's in those three words that I hope this book will make an impact in your life. That has been my charge - my purpose. It took me a long time to know and understand it, not the "why" but the "just is" about it. Only a handful of people "get me" and are excited for me, anyway.

Most people think I'm nuts for walking away two different times from a lucrative nursing career to give back and encourage others, to listen to that whisper inside of me urging me on.

It's my hope that I have been urged on *for you*. This journey for me has been intensely personal and spiritual. I hope it has awakened something in you.

Have you been encouraged by the knowledge that any one of us at any time can make a difference in some one else's life, if we are available? That's all it takes - just being available. Because all of us have great gifts, talents and subtle nuances that belong only to us, but if shared - can produce incredible results with magnificent portraits of lives changed.

Have you been encouraged to know that since your life is like a painting it is not finished yet? So baby, you still have a lot of blank canvas to cover! Your canvas is just waiting for you to take brush in hand, dip it in some paint and start dabbing away - broad vivid strokes and light, feathery delicate wisps with splotches of rich color.

Oh heck, just throw the whole paint can at it and squish it around with your hands if you want to. It's your painting!

It's your life - make it count! And never throw your can of paint away.

Pay attention!

There is no failure unless you don't try. You only fail if you never get in the game and play.

Have you been empowered by knowing that you were made perfectly just as you are, warts and all? Because they are your warts and they were put there because they have a purpose, same as you have a purpose. Your purpose is to use those warts and change someone's life.

And watch out, it just might be your own!

The empowerment is that you don't have to know everything or have everything to start doing what your heart tells you to do. *Just start doing, the rest will show up.* Everything we want starts with a move from *us*. It may be a thought only or maybe a thought and an action. And remember, that is why the rest of the world is here, to make dreams come true.

So, don't take no for an answer.

Don't let anyone tell you that you are not good enough or smart enough or you are "less than". It is in our weaknesses and our frailties that we can walk in-spirit and accomplish great things *because* we are not alone. We have a whole army of soldiers or scientists or tillers of the ground or whatever we need at that moment to stand with us and give us the courage, support, confidence and security we need to step up and step out.

Just do it! But, *"do it true"*.

That's a profound statement. It's not enough just to do it, you must do it true to yourself. You are not your mother, your father, your sister or the prom queen (who you secretly hated). You are you and there is only one of you. And only *you* can live out your divine purpose and only *you* can live in *your full potential*.

And you can, you will. You must!

It's probably a really good thing that here *is* only one of me.

So, do it scared, but just do it!

There is nothing wrong with being scared. If we aren't at least a little scared then we haven't thought about the consequences of what we are about to undertake. But don't think too long, you may talk yourself out of it. Just think long enough so you don't jump out of a plane without a parachute, or actually shoot someone and not just say you feel like doing it.

Be bold and courageous!

If you feel you are too scared it's just your ego getting in the way. Egos are a real pain, they like to be in charge but in reality they are just big "fraidy cats". They want others to write that book you are dreaming about writing or that painting you have always wanted to paint or that career you long to go after. Your ego wants others to do it because it wants to be smarter than you and have something to hold over your head. You know what I mean, "Na, na, nana, na..." But, *you* are bigger and smarter and more creative than your ego.

YOU are in charge!

So do it scared and then feel the wonder. Feel the confidence that immediately follows. That feeling of *extraordinaire* that rushes over you. It is awesome!

So do it!

Have you been engaged by knowing you are the mirror of truth in which God shines his perfect light?

So, then let it shine, baby!

You deserve it and so do others. They deserve to see your light shining, so let it shine really bright. Split the darkness with it!

Illuminate your whole block, your whole neighborhood, your whole town!

And why stop there?

Remember this principle: *Shine your light, your light bumps into someone, it lights them up, they start to shine, then their light travels and bumps into someone else, their light shines and so on, and so on, and so on...*

Your light has the power to light up the world!

O-N-E - can make a difference!

In fact, "o-n-e" can make *all* the difference.

One is the difference...

It's like imaging that you are a big magnet, the most powerful magnet in the world - only in reverse. Instead of attracting things to you, you are sending out things that get stuck to other people.

Boy, there were times I wish I could stick some cream pies right into the faces of a couple people – ha, ha, ha.

All joking aside, I love this idea of a reverse magnet. Think about it, when you give a compliment you get a smile or a blush in return. Hopefully that good feeling they have will rub off and stick to someone else and the beat goes on. But when you insult someone what happens? It hurts them, it sticks to them and then to get it off of themselves they either have to bury it down deep or they sling it back at someone. Maybe that person is you or maybe it's just some innocent bystander.

Hasn't that happened to you before?

You are just standing there minding your own darn business and "wham" you get hit with a "curve ball ugly", as I call them. But what if we practiced sending out good signals, rays of sunshine, blessings, kind words and deeds and forgiveness? All those good things would be sticking to people out there. It might be the first person just innocently standing around who is in your line of fire. Or maybe it is someone you have specifically targeted and you take aim at them and fire a big whopper of love, instead of slapstick comedy. It would be slapstick LOVE!

Haven't you ever just walked up to someone in the grocery store and said, "Gee, that's a pretty sweater, it's a great color on you." I don't care if it's the ugliest sweater you have ever seen and the color makes you want to vomit. Do it! You will make their day. It could be the difference between them feeling like a toad with warts and feeling like a prince or princess. You just changed someone's life today and it only took a second of your time. It didn't cost any money, it didn't cost you anything. And maybe, just maybe – you are the one who will reap the biggest reward!

I think I am going to buy a white T-shirt and get a big, fat red magic marker and write all over the shirt, *"Look at me, I am the biggest reverse magnet in the universe!"*

Look out!

I might be calling you for bail money.

Hey, that would make a good reality show, too - a show about a bail bondsman who goes around saying and doing spontaneously-outrageous kind things for people and then has to bail them self out of jail for disturbing the peace or disturbing the "un-peace".

We can call it "Peaceless" or "Priceless" or "Peace at a Price".

Truth is truth no matter if you believe it or not.

Ironically, I see this as both comforting and annoying. Comforting because I don't have to decipher what is truth and what is not truth, and annoying because I want to be in control.

I wonder, how do we prepare for the desert?

I mean we all will experience deserts in our life. There is no escaping that, but how do you really prepare for one? Is it a matter of learning to survive in the desert, maybe practicing hard times or barren times to come? Or is it getting so fat on life and what it has to offer that when the desert comes we can live off the fat and hope the fat lasts long enough to outlive the desert before we starve. What do you think?

What's a cactus to do?

In the past I have tried curtain #1 - practicing hard times. I don't recommend it. Since you have to go through the desert anyway later on - why waste time with a run-through? That's like *double* agony!

Now that I have given myself permission to be "enlightened" regarding this, I am going to try what's behind curtain #2 - gobble up a fattened life. Gobble, gobble, gobble!

All things work for the good of someone.

I picture life as this 200 pound lump of granite. Everyone who is born gets to start out with their own 200 pound lump. Try to picture that one in your head. My lump is smooth and shiny with several big, jagged edges and it looks like a rainbow of variegated grays speckled with white dots. *Got it?*

Everyday some of the rough edges are chipped away as I am molded into the creation I was always meant to be. The master sculptor chisels that granite and then uses a pumice stone to make me smooth and to polish me until I glow and shine for all to see.

How about you? What does your lump look like?

Are you still full of jagged rough edges or have you let your master sculptor lovingly turn you into a work of art? Or are you still buried in the ground or *under the ground*?

Hey, get up and dig yourself out!

Hurry - times a wasting, or times a ticking – either way, you are wasting something.

You may need to start with baby steps before you grow with leaps and bounds and that's okay. That's what is great about life; it's a "do at your own pace" remedial school. And if you don't get it right the first time, believe me the experience will come back again and again. It actually will haunt you until to learn or conquer what ever it is that you are supposed to.

Stay connected to your loved ones. Make a bucket list and actually do the items on the list, don't just complain why you can't do them. Do the hobbies you love, paint those pictures and be the creative force in your own life. If you are a list maker, schedule in fun and creative time and just plain old "goof-off" time. You need it!

And if you schedule it you won't feel so guilty actually doing it. So, if you are a Type-A personality, and if it's on your list, then you *have* to do it.

You will make yourself do every thing on that stupid list! Trust me.

I did just that this morning and I discovered something remarkable. I had made my list (I am so anal I do it the night before), and had scheduled 30 minutes of pleasure reading. Now that could mean almost anything - any article, book, email, billboard or "wanted" poster at the post office, What I read was an email from a friend. It was about the Seven Wonders of the World, it goes like this:

A teacher asked her grade school class to name the "Seven Wonders of the World". The students all excitedly starting talking and shouting out answers until they came up with the final list of seven wonders. The normal things were there; the Pyramids, the Grand Canyon, the Great Wall of China... you get the picture.

It was then the teacher noticed that one of her students had not been participating but was writing fervently on his paper. She stood behind him and looked down at what he had written, stared at it for several minutes with her head bowed and then, quietly sat behind her desk. This is what he wrote as his Seven Wonders of the World:

<u>To see</u> - a beautiful sunset
<u>To smell</u> - the roses in my grandma's yard
<u>To hear</u> - the birds singing
<u>To taste</u> - a chocolate ice cream cone
<u>To talk</u> - to my brother and share a secret
<u>To walk</u> - the neighbor's dog
<u>To love</u> - everyone.

What would have been your answer?

Today is precious, make it count!

I like that. I need those kinds of "kicks" in the pants. In fact, I pray for them in my life to happen and I always try to remember when they do. I make a note of it or journal it as "important" in some way. It reminds me that my angel just gave me a nudge - keeping me on my *path of purpose.*

Confession time, I must confess there is an addendum to this contract of healthy eating and healthy lifestyle I talked about earlier. Once in a while you need to cheat. You must! That's also in the contract, here's an example why.

It is such an incredibly awesome day. It's late September - upper 60's, sunny with big white billowy clouds racing across the sky, making me feel so alive and happy to be on planet earth today. The leaves are changing and hues of gold, orange and red are whirling and swirling around me as the wind catches them, suspends them in mid air and then makes a circus all over the cobblestone path with them.

Feeling invincible and totally enjoying the youthful spring in my step and the crisp clean air surging all through my body, I passed the Sweets and Ice Cream Shoppe and my little 6 ½ sized shoes turned me around. Before I knew what had happened I was holding a luxurious heaping scoop of cinnamon crumb ice cream which was now dripping down the sugar cone - *and my hand.*

It was beautiful!

So, after I paid for my work of art, the clerk at the counter smiled, winked at me and then said, "Have a deliciously wicked day!"

Absolutely! And I did.

Have I revolutionized you?

Has any of my remembering and my ramblings felt like revolutionary thinking to you?

Oh, I do hope so. The last thing I want to be is boring.

I want to be relevant to your needs and what is going on in your life now. And in doing so, being relative I mean, I want to boldly tell you that I think harmony has gotten a bad rap. It's probably the old stale leftovers from the "hippie and flower-child days" when peace and love and "living in harmony" was "ruining the country", so said the soothsayers of the establishment.

But I don't mean harmony like some may envision - long-haired free-spirits with glazed-over looks in their eyes wasting away the day floating on some pink cloud or "magic carpet ride". I am talking about the harmony that takes a lot of work, and true harmony does. It will wear you out trying to get your mind, your body, your soul, your heart and your thoughts to all work together for your greater good.

Think about it and then try it. See if you can do it. See if you think it is so easy. Anyone who thinks it's easy is faking it. You have to pay attention, not something that us humans do naturally. But I am convinced that it's our harmony that enables us to reach our full potential and to encounter ourselves - as we work out our divine purpose.

Ah, life... life? *Life!*

And if it's our harmony that moves us towards the light, lightens our load and helps us catch a glimpse of our true likeness - then what does the harmony in us to do to others? Life is cause and effect and "special effects", the bigger the better.

So, when was the last time you examined a leaf?

Susan, did your mind just do one of those skipping things like when you are listening to your favorite CD and it starts making that weird "every third word noise" and suddenly you are in the middle of the next song?

"No, my mind is just fine thank you very much."

Oh-oh, I think I am holding that conversation again with myself.

I want to know, have you ever examined one? A leaf, I mean.

Have you held one in your hand and stared at it for at least five minutes. No two leaves are exactly the same, you know. They may be very close, but not duplicates - their shapes and colors, their stems and veins, their softness and pliability or their dried roughness. Their beauty and their imperfections - they each have their own imprint.

I believe that's how it is with all of us.

When we interact with people we leave an imprint on them. We leave part of ourselves with them. It doesn't matter if we have known someone for a long time or just an accidental "brush up against" someone, we leave our imprint – a little bit of our personality with them, like the leaf. And the more interaction or "brushing up against" that someone gets the more leaves they have to protect them and cushion their fall.

It's almost as if God takes a deep breath and blows all these leaves around them (around you) – surrounding you and wrapping you in a cocoon, an incubator of love.

Hmmm...

Almost makes you feel like you just ate a warm chocolate chip cookie, doesn't it?

So, go out and deposit your leaves. Go leave, or is that leaf? Leave your imprint and be part of a big pile of leaves that someone out there needs to fall into as they tumble and hope to find a soft place to land.

Maybe you are part of a big thick warm blanket of leaves cuddling and caressing someone with love and encouragement. Or maybe you are part of a meadow full of brightly-colored dancing leaves just waiting for someone to come and play and giggle and laugh...

Whatever your *leaf destination* is, your *"leaf calling"*, go forth and leaf!

Give out and pour out, give them away. Don't deposit them in the bank, bury them or try to store up your "leaf-nuts" like squirrels do before winter.

These leaves don't work like that!

Remember to read the instructions. leaves will dry up and blow away if not used properly.

So, leave your trail of leaves behind you!

Happy trails to you...

Read on...

Epilogue

I just got done watching a program on television about brain scans and neuro marketing. Most of you are probably wondering way I would be telling you this now, in a section entitled "Epilogue". It's okay, I don't' blame you for wondering. It means you are questioning, you aren't just taking these words at face value - your brain is active. You are being *intentional*.

First let me tell you about the program and then I will explain the "why".

Ever since my counselor, Claire, years ago turned me on to PET scans and the ways our brains change, I have been fascinated. I have been hooked. Every time there is a program or article pertaining to this subject I try to read it or watch it. This one used Alan Alda, the actor, as one of the subjects. You know, Hawkeye Pearce from "MASH". Anyway, what stood out to me was the experiment where they showed Alan Alda (and others) pictures of common items anyone would buy - such as sun glasses, cars, appliances, etc... Then he was asked to rate them on whether he thought they were cool or not cool.

Sounds simple, maybe even boring, but here is the fascinating thing. You would think our brains would "light up" or show more intensity for the things people thought were cool. But this was only true for some of the test subjects. The opposite was true for the rest. Their brains "lit up" with more intensity for the things they thought were *not cool*.

How cool is that?

Sorry, I couldn't resist that. My brain couldn't stop my fingers from typing it.

What does it mean? It means we are all wired differently, that some people find pleasure more intense and others find "dislike" more powerful.

Hmmm... no wonder we can't get along. No wonder relationships are so hard. No wonder...

The next experiment was just as revealing. Most of us think we know how we feel and what we think about life, people and things in general. So because of that we figure we know how we will react to others and treat others. I believe most of us want to believe we are unbiased, non-prejudicial and fair. We don't want to think we have hidden agendas and hidden prejudices lurking down deep somewhere.

Well, I believe they used Alan Alda as a test subject because he is quite well-known for his open mindedness and for being a feminist. They did several different experiments with him. One was a word association test which started out easy and gradually became more and more complicated, using groupings of words. And, by the end of the experiment there was no way to manipulate it - deep dark feelings were activated and revealed.

Another was a multiple choice question and answer test. But it got tricky, it would show a negative or distasteful picture of a people group and then the question following would be about that people group. They also reversed the process, using positive or humanitarian-like pictures and then asking a question about that people group. And lastly, there were the questions with answers without the pictures first - to round out the experiment. Results were; the pictures affected (biased) just about everyone, some more and some less than others – even Alan Alda. *No one was immune.*

So what, who cares?

Well, you better start caring because they talked about how information like this has sparked a new type of marketing - neuro marketing. I know sales, advertising and marketing people have always tried to think of ways to get us to buy their products. Heck, I have done marketing and sales myself and put together ads and brochures. So I am well aware of how I was trying to motivate my audience. And I know you may be thinking this is all harmless and so what if this stuff is used to try to get people to buy their next car or cell phone?

Again you ask, "Why should I be fascinated?" or, "Why is this important to me?"

Well, it's not just about the car or the phone. What if it's about the next President of the United States? What's if it's about euthanasia? What's if it's about who deserves a job or food or life-saving medication?

Try reading research on mobs. Not like "The Mob" in the "Godfather", but the kind of mob that starts riots. It will frighten you. I challenge you to just watch the news now with a more open mind. Take a day or a week and get out a sheet of paper and really start to pay attention. Write down every time you feel yourself being manipulated into thinking or buying something that you normally wouldn't. Count it up after that day or that week. Surprised? Look for the neuro marketing, *it's everywhere.*

Pay attention. Don't think your voice doesn't count.

There is an awesome song by Barry Manilow entitled, "One Voice". I hope you will look it up on the internet or better still go buy it. The lyrics, combined with the music and Barry's brilliant way of delivering a song, will inspire you. It should, if it doesn't - you don't have a heartbeat and you better check your pulse.

Have you figured out yet why I am talking about all of this here and now?

One more hint. Let's use me as the example.

As I began remembering who I was, I found out that in my early years I played a very active role in my life. I paid attention to everything, to details, to the small stuff, the little things – *the important things*. Nothing much was missed. I talked about current events, read all the time, spoke out against things I thought were unjust and I was a leader. Then something happened to me. This almost radical kind of person disappeared and Person #2 took over. I mean it wasn't a "coo" or big battle that took place, one day I was just that other person.

I didn't recognize it. It was like I fell asleep one night and the next morning I was "the other", like in the movie about the pods. I stopped reading and watching the news. I stopped caring about world events. I stopped questioning and fighting for my beliefs. I don't know if I got tired or lazy or if I stopped believing I could make a difference. It doesn't matter. It's not about the "whys'. We waste too much time talking about the "whys". We just need to start "doing". This was a lost period in my life. I can't remember too much of it. It was like mashed potatoes with no salt or butter, bland and forgettable.

Gradually I began waking up, like I was coming out of a coma. But I didn't fully awaken for years. It was only recently that I realized I was fully alive again and had been sandblasted out of my cement shoes and catapulted into the land of the living again. Now I make sure everyday is a day of discovery. Reading books just for the pleasure of it not because I must do it for a job or for a test, meditating and paying attention to sounds and colors, walking in nature, making sure I do at least one thing a day just for me - a gift to myself.

Marking my territory is the way I like to look at it.

It's like when I take my dog Tillie on a walk. She prances and skips. Yes, she skips when she is really happy. And she sniffs. She sniffs everything and when she sniffs another dog's "left behinds" she pees there and makes it *her territory*. She marks her territory!

So that is what I have decided a goal for me will be, to daily mark my territory - so I won't forget again. I won't forget how wonderful life can be just breathing, breathing it all in. This is what I want you to see. This is why talking about our brains is so important. We all must pay attention and seek out information and look for experiences so we can question and speak out. Make noise and remember to make a difference and never let life just happen to us! If you do this then you haven't given up. So no giving up! No matter what fruit life gives you, make lemonade!

Get up and stand up for what you believe in! Stand up for what is important to you!

Do you *know* what is important to you? What will you die for? But more importantly, *what will you live for*? *Living* takes a lot of effort.

*What are **you** willing to live for*?

Hmmm... got your juices going, didn't I? Lemonade anyone?

I have a very strange condition. I am an both insider and outsider at the same time. It is quite maddening to others and am starting not to like it much myself. I used to think it was a good thing to have. But I now realize that it has contributed to my inability to experience great joy and has resulted in not having very many "natural highs" in my life. Instead of feeling outraged or happy beyond words when it would have been normal to do so, I was outside myself instead, and not feeling it.

I had stepped outside myself and had become an outsider to my own experience. At first I thought I was just putting myself in the other person's shoes or examining it from another perspective. You know, like a scientist would do. But I am not a scientist or genius material. It was my way of protecting myself.

So now for me, this coming of age and re-awakening has pointed out things I need to change. Things I didn't realize I needed to change. This "insider-outsider" thing is one of them, and everyday now I intentionally refuse to allow myself to fall back into sleepwalking habits.

If you are one of these insider-outsider people, dump it! Don't let it interfere with who you truly are supposed to be!

If I made these statements to you: "We have the power to choose", "We have no choice" and "Both are true" would you believe me? Would I be right?

What if I said they happened simultaneously? Would that make a difference? What if I said that even when we make a choice that choice was just a step along our path which has been written for us already? And that we, human beings, are just willing but unknowing participants in this play that we call life?

What if a choice was no choice at all?

Okay, this is where I think I need to stop the stimulation and bring the focus back. So I will call this, "the jumping off place". Because I have these thoughts every day and I could go on and on - so it's time for me to just "jump off".

My hope in sharing this with you is to bring kindred spirits together, awaken some dead wood and shake out the numbness.

I write like I think and speak and I hope this feels as natural to you as it does for me. I had to use *my* voice because there is someone who needs to hear it just as it is written. And even if it was for just that *one person,* it has been worth it. Because if we are all connected by spirit through frequency via magnetic force or wavelength then, what touches one - truly touches all.

You may have noticed that there seems to be three distinct parts to this book, other than the beginning, middle and end of course. The distinction I believe is that the first several chapters are the coming out of my emotions part. It's a little irreverent in places and unusual but it was as I was experiencing it. These chapters are my ramblings and my rawness. They represent me realizing I was at the bottom of a very, very deep well and there was no one to help me out. I had to fumble to find the rope and begin to pull myself up one inch at a time.

The middle part of the book was the remembering part. Once I had pulled myself out of the well it was important to pause and take stock of where I was, where I had been and how I had gotten from there to here and contemplate where my life was headed.

The last part, the third distinction, is the plan. It's the plan so I (or now you), never have to fall back and be in that deep, dark well again. And the best part, the really good part - it's not the end of the story. It's never the end of the story! The rest of my story is too important to just have put it here, as an add-on, something trailing behind. It would have robbed it of its power. It would have dulled its brilliance.

The rest of the story is about the women.

But, there is such a high intensity to the stories of these remarkable women that it must be told nakedly and honestly, standing alone without blemish. So, if you have found these chapters wondrous, I believe you will find the next segment illuminating and inspirational. Not only do I spend time breaking down how the program itself works and how it works on every aspect of these ladies' lives – but you get to find out what happens with Tom and I, it's in there too.

See, there's still a little bit of soap opera in me, a little touch of drama. I can't help it! I mean, I'm still a woman after all and I'm still breathing.

I've named the next book, "Matchmaker – The Perfect Match". Again, it will be bubbling over with heart and soul, and truth. So now...

I hope I have done my job. I hope I have served my purpose. If I have, you will "pay it forward" and give this book to someone. If I have, you will purchase "Matchmaker" or through the power of your thoughts bring about the realization of "Matchmaker" in your life. How's that?

Don't forget what we seek after, like buried treasure, we will find. It will become our next life story. Make it a good one!

Make it a rich one!

Why?

I am a shell.
A shell of a person,
Or is it a metamorphosis I seek?
Betwixt and between, what's outside and what's in.
Like a M & M with a hard candy shell,
Locking in that precious softness and flavor.
Make me full of all the flavors and colors of life.
Time is of no matter,
Today I want the hidden chocolate treasure.
And make my yesterdays - the shell.

- Susan Farah

P.S. If you have read this far and realized that you too feel as if you have lived in a hurricane, that you have hidden yourself away from the world or have named your "blind spot" and *it is you* – then we must be related. Maybe we are second or third cousins.

So cuz, I look forward to getting to know you further and spending time with you. Let's you and I journey and journal together and exquisitely find out "who" we are and then help others do the same.

So, until next time...

It's been my pleasure!

Susan

APPENDIX ONE

Things that must be done before program opens

Initial – start-up of non-profit

Determine name of program (corporation) and become incorporated

To do the above must have board of directors in place

Be careful how you set up your by-laws and who you chose to be on your board

Individuals with money sound great but you can't do all the work so you want a "working board" committed to raising money and raising awareness

Hold regular meetings and document well

All decisions of weight must be approved by board

If you are the person "in charge" of this "cruise ship" (non-profit) make sure this is spelled out in your by-laws and your authority is very clear

Obtain 501c3

To do the above you must know the purpose of your non-profit – this will determine everything from this point on

Before you accept your first dollar as a 501c3 you must have a bank account and the structure in place to account for all donations (recommend a CPA)

Choose your bank wisely and have someone counter-sign checks with you – must have appropriate paper trail for all monies coming in and going out

As a 501c3 - everything you do and say will come under high scrutiny from the government, from the community and from every donor

Remember- you must have a receipt for everything you buy or work that is done which you are paying for - if a friend or relative is the person you have chosen (you must show why that person was chosen - ie - job bids or a vote from your board)

There can be no question that the money you have raised is being spent properly - you will lose your donors, your reputation and finally the 501c3 if you do not follow the rules

Develop a brochure or packet of information to hand out when you talk to people about your non-profit (program)

Develop website

Start sending out a monthly newsletter

Develop a receipt thank-you letter to give to donors (include tax-id number)

Go out and raise money - remember YOU must be 100% committed to your vision and be able to articulate to others - otherwise they will not believe you

Have you done your research? Be accurate in all you say and do. You must be credible - your program must be credible

Know how much money it will take to do the purpose of your non-profit

If you can "do" your program, or can do the "essence" of your program while raising the initial monies - great! Even if it is to refer people to other established programs - you are still helping the people you have determined your non-profit is committed to help

Now this is where we come to the fork in the road

If your vision is not residential - then continuing to do the above - because this is your vision

But if your purpose is to have a residential program, helping individuals while housing and feeding them, then read on...

APPENDIX TWO

Knowing the type and purpose for your residential center will be crucial to how you proceed from this point on; here are just some of the reasons why:
- Zoning
- Category your residential home falls into so you can comply with city, county, state and federal laws and their inspections (start with fire marshal)
- Licensing or certification of staff, program, etc...

Since my direct experience is with developing and opening a 14-bed residential program for individuals with life-controlling problems – this is where the rest of Appendix Two will lead us –

Question to ask – Are you going to be independent or are you going to be a part of a state, national or international group?

Each has their pros and cons. Only you can determine what you have been "called" to do in your heart. YOU are the captain of your destiny and the destiny of your 501c3. You have to KNOW what is true so you can stay on course. You will get advice (solicited and non-solicited) and you must be able to sift through it and know the difference between what is right for your program and what is wrong for your program. Only YOU will know this – you have to take the responsibility and the accountability for it – good or bad. The buck stops with YOU! It has to or, you will not succeed.

So the real question to ask is – Are you ready?

If you still reading then you have chosen "Yes, I am ready!"

So brave one, here goes:

Call the fire marshal – explain what you want to do, he will determine your next step. His answer to you will involve – zoning, location, number of individuals you can house, staff you can house, ADA requirements, the need for a sprinkler system, adequate parking, etc... Knowing all this BEFORE you look for a location is critical

Find out if what you want to do will require a license from the state or any special certified or licensed staff. If part of your source for funding will be city, county, state or federal money – it is a high probability you are going to have to jump through some hoops to get it (it starts here).

Do your homework – do your research on the front end of this project. I know you want to get in there and DO! But if you just start delivering the program and haven't fully developed it or find out what you must have to do it and also find out what you can and cannot legally do – I might have to come and bail you out of jail!

If you have done everything I have asked up to this point and you still are determined to continue because you believe you must – because you have a vision that cannot be denied. Because there are hurting people out there who you must help. Because you can't sleep, or eat or even breathe until you do it – go to Appendix Three

APPENDIX THREE

Determine the physical needs of your center: staff bedrooms, client bedrooms, bathrooms, classroom, dining room, living room, offices, counseling/meeting room, laundry room, pantry and storage

Pick your location. Think this one through! Location is everything.

What else will you need?
Alarms on doors/windows
Locks on staff/office door
The only telephone will be locked up in the office (staff can carry a cell phone)
Need locked medication cabinet & money lock-up
Need sheets, towels, containers for toiletries, dishes, silverware, pots and pans, small appliances, bedspreads/ blankets, furniture, bunk beds, TV for video's, DVD's, cassette players for CD's and or tapes
Need copier, computer for office, office supplies, classroom supplies – paper, pens
Meet all codes, restrictions and pass all inspections
Must be handicapped assessable
Need cleaning and paper products

At this point you should have prayed, researched and decided on what your program will offer, the curriculum and other services the individuals will receive while they are there

(ie - medical care, dental and eye care, job skills, parenting classes, music, art, vocational training, exercise, special diets, leadership opportunities, internships opportunities, mission trips, recreational therapy/fun, etc...)

Put your program down in writing along with your curriculum and purchase all the books and materials needed to deliver the program

How will you know when a person is done with the program - what is your criteria for graduation? Speaking of graduation - make it a celebration and decide all the things you will do to mark the occasion

Have you worked with the family - remember sometimes they get as sick or needy as the individual you are working with

Develop the rule book and staff rule book

Make copies of classroom rules and curriculum, contracts, rule books, admissions paperwork, admission packets, staff hand books and daily schedules

Hire and train staff (need live-in staff) make sure your staff have the same values, beliefs and want the same outcomes as you do

Need someone to watch them 24-7 and live-in
Need someone to oversee kitchen, buy food and make menus
Need classroom teacher/monitor to grade and interpret homework
Need someone to assign & monitor work duties
Need staff to mentor/counsel time

Develop budget and work out student fees, what ministry will provide and what students need to provide

Is this you? No regular TV or music, Christian videos/DVDs/CDs-no computers, radios cell phones or cars, no mail delivered to the house (PO Box)

Develop system to have medication and money and valuables locked up and monitored

Set up monitoring of phone calls, letters/visits

Make sure on admission student and family read rules, consequences and sign they understand

Develop a way of tracking your students after they have left or graduated (make sure you tell the wonderful successes of those who have graduated)

Do you want to have an alumni program, newsletter, banquets?

Vehicles – what do you need - remember to log mileage – all vehicles

Finish getting house as it needs to be, landscape outside

Do you want a sign out front? Be in the phone book? Hotlines? - how will you market your services?

Make a wish list to give to donors – ex. need exercise room, second laundry room

Optional - develop computer program for students and outfit (open to community?)

Optional - add Graduate House – last phase of program (most of all the above will need to be done for this)

Ongoing – fundraise - book rallies, rehearse testimonies, rehearse singing-choir, do video, do a banquet, work on grants, do car washes, walk-a-thons, bike-a-thons, raffles, auctions, golf tournaments

Do "Support-a-student" program – where donors pledge $____ a month to help sponsor a student

Get involved with local churches – for donations, volunteers, gifts for holidays

Get involved with local college, vocational school and grade and high schools - special projects, fund-raisers and gifts for the holidays Do you have local celebrities? Do you have local people who have "overcome" the situation your students are in?

Contact United Way, city or country foundations, city council or county commissioners, utility companies, local newspapers, magazines, radio station and cable channel

Remember to have regular meetings with your board, get them involved and TAKE GOOD MINUTES AND RECORD THEM IN A BOOK

Pay your bills on time!

Be open, honest and ASK for what you need! Remember you are not asking for yourself - you are asking for the people you are helping

The list is endless - and will go on as long as your program/ ministry does

And then there is all the stuff I have forgotten to tell you or that pops up its ugly head!

GOOD LUCK!

Biography

Susan Farah is an author, pastor, life empowerment coach and founder of **Ex3 = Encourage Empower Engage** – a leadership and coaching consultation program. Building on twenty-eight years of nurturing, creating winning teams and healing work environments, Susan strives to successfully bring individuals to their fullest potential. Combining coaching, mentoring and individualized life goal-setting, lives are transformed and empowered.

Her book, "So" is her second published and her first written attempt in a series of inspiring books and poems. "27 E Words That Will Change Your Life" was published in July 2013. Susan lives in Blowing Rock, North Carolina with her husband Tom and their spunky dog, Tillie.